The BIG LOUISIANA Reproducible Activity Book!

BY CAROLE MARSH

This activity book has material which correlates with Louisiana's Social Studies Content Standards.

At every opportunity, we have tried to relate information to the History and Social Science, English, Science, Math, Civics, Economics, and Computer Technology SSCS directives.

For additional information, go to our website: **www.gallopade.com**

Published by
GALLOPADE™ INTERNATIONAL
800-536-2GET
www.gallopade.com

TECH CONNECTS

Connect to a world of related information, activities, and more at:
www.gallopade.com/techconnects.html
password: activity

Gallopade is proud to be a member or supporter of these educational organizations and associations:

ASCD™ · ABA American Booksellers Association · Association of Partners for Public Lands · NCSS

A Word From The Author

Louisiana is a very special state. Almost everything about Louisiana is interesting and fun! It has a remarkable history that helped create the great nation of America. Louisiana enjoys an amazing geography of incredible beauty and fascination. The state's people are unique and have accomplished many great things.

This Activity Book is chockful of activities to entice you to learn more about Louisiana. While completing mazes, dot-to-dots, word searches, coloring activities, word codes, and other fun-to-do activities, you'll learn about Louisiana's history, geography, people, places, animals, legends, and more.

Whether you're sitting in a classroom, stuck inside on a rainy day, or–better yet–sitting in the back seat of a car touring the wonderful state of Louisiana, my hope is that you have as much fun using this Activity Book as I did writing it.

Enjoy your Louisiana Experience–it's the trip of a lifetime!!

Carole Marsh

The Louisiana Experience Series

My First Pocket Guide to Louisiana!

The Big Louisiana Reproducible Activity Book

The Louisiana Coloring Book!

My First Book About Louisiana!

Louisiana Jeopardy: Answers & Questions About Our State

Louisiana "Jography!": A Fun Run Through Our State

The Louisiana Experience! Sticker Pack

The Louisiana Experience! Poster/Map

Discover Louisiana CD-ROM

Louisiana "GEO" Bingo Game

Louisiana "HISTO" Bingo Game

Louisiana "BIO" Bingo Game

Louisiana Millionaire GameBook

Louisiana Wheel of Fortune GameBook

Louisiana Survivor GameBook

Color Me!
Louisiana
Brown
Like the eastern brown pelican
Brown
BLUE
Like the Gulf of Mexico
Blue
YELLOW
Like fresh corn
Yellow
RED
Like boiled crawfish
Red
Black
BLACK
Like the stripes on a honeybee
Purple
PURPLE
Like the native Violet
Green
GREEN
Like mossy swamps
Orange
ORANGE
Like the setting sun

The Louisiana Experience Series

My First Pocket Guide to Louisiana!

The Big Louisiana Reproducible Activity Book

The Louisiana Coloring Book!

My First Book About Louisiana!

Louisiana Jeopardy: Answers & Questions About Our State

Louisiana "Jography!": A Fun Run Through Our State

The Louisiana Experience! Sticker Pack

The Louisiana Experience! Poster/Map

Discover Louisiana CD-ROM

Louisiana "GEO" Bingo Game

Louisiana "HISTO" Bingo Game

Louisiana "BIO" Bingo Game

Louisiana Millionaire GameBook

Louisiana Wheel of Fortune GameBook

Louisiana Survivor GameBook

Color Me!
Louisiana
Brown
Like the eastern brown pelican
BLUE
Like the Gulf of Mexico
YELLOW
Like fresh corn
RED
Like boiled crawfish
BLACK
Like the stripes on a honeybee
PURPLE
Like the native Violet
GREEN
Like mossy swamps
ORANGE
Like the setting sun

Our State Bird!

Connect the dots to see Louisiana's beautiful state bird, the eastern brown pelican.

When you are done, color the bird.

Write the bird's name in the space below.

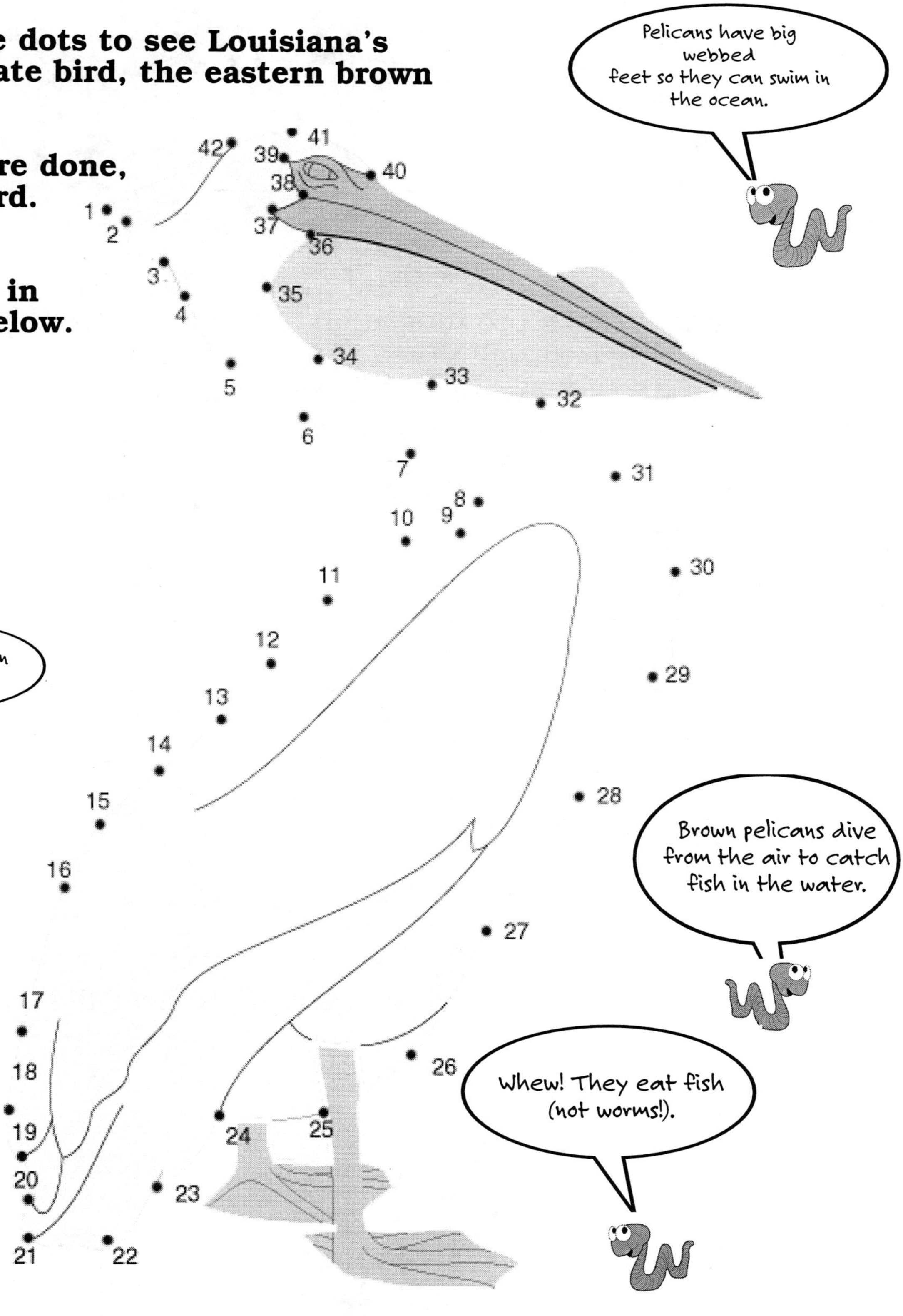

_ _

Cajun Country

In 1755, a group of French colonists in Acadia (Nova Scotia) were EXILED by the British. They refused to give up their religion, and so they had to leave Acadia. Many of them RELOCATED south to Louisiana. They built farms and fishing villages on the rivers and bayous. The word "Cajun" comes from the original French pronunciation of Acadian – "A-ca-jan."

Today, Cajun country EXTENDS from the Gulf coast to the central part of Louisiana. Cajuns are famous for their UNIQUE food. Dishes like jambalaya, gumbo, and crawfish pie are DISTINCTLY Cajun.

See if you can figure out the meanings of these words from the story above.

1. exiled:____

2. relocated:______________________________________

3. extends:_______________________________________

4. unique:____

5. distinctly:______________________________________

Now, check your answers in a dictionary. How close did you get?

Louisiana! All Around Bubblegram

Bubble up on your knowledge of Louisiana's bordering states and bodies of water.

Fill in the bubblegram by using the clues below.

1. A state north of Louisiana
2. A state east of Louisiana
3. A body of water south of Louisiana
4. The largest lake in Louisiana
5. A state west of Louisiana
6. The capital of Louisiana

1. ___ ___ ___ ___ ◯ ___ ___ ___

2. ___ ___ ___ ___ ___ ___ ___ ◯ ___ ___ ◯

3. ___ ◯ ___ ___ ___ ◯ ___ ___ ___ ___ ___ ◯ ___

4. ___ ◯ ◯ ___ ◯ ___ ___ ___ ___ ___ ___ ___ ◯

5. ___ ◯ ___ ___ ___

6. ___ ___ ___ ___ ◯ ___ ◯ ___ ___ ◯

Now unscramble the "bubble" letters to complete Louisiana's motto!

___ ___ ___ ___ ___, JUSTICE, ___ ___ ___ ___ ___ D ___ ___ ___ ___

ANSWERS: 1.ARKANSAS 2.MISSISSIPPI 3.GULF OF MEXICO 4.PONTCHARTRAIN 5.TEXAS 6.BATON ROUGE
MYSTERY MOTTO: UNION, JUSTICE, CONFIDENCE

Symbols of the United States

These are some of the symbols that remind us of America. We show these symbols honor and respect.

Color each symbol.

American Flag

Statue of Liberty

Bald Eagle

Liberty Bell

Cajun Cuisine

Because Louisiana is on the Gulf of Mexico, many Cajun dishes use seafood as a main ingredient. Spicy stews called gumbos can be made from shrimp. Thick soups called bisques are made with many kinds of seafood, and they even make crawfish pie! What's your favorite Cajun dish?

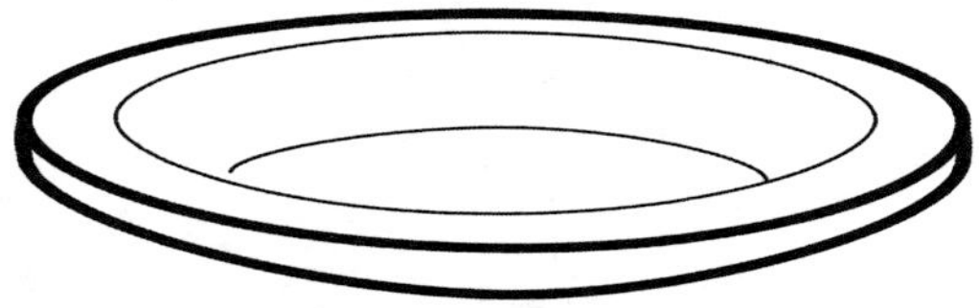

How many spoons are on the page? ☐

How many forks are on the page? ☐

How many dishes are on the page? ☐

Color the spoons, forks, and dishes.

ANSWERS: 5 spoons 7 forks 5 dishes

Louisiana Wheel of Fortune, Indian Style!

The names of Louisiana's many Native American Indian tribes contain enough consonants to play . . . Wheel of Fortune!

See if you can figure out the Wheel of Fortune-style puzzles below! "Vanna" has given you some of the consonants in each word.

C H _ _ _ _ _ C H _

_ T _ K _ P _

C _ D D _

N _ T _ _ _ T _ _ _ _ _

_ _ T _ S _

_ D _ _

C _ _ C _ _ _

ANSWERS: CHITIMACHA ATAKAPA CADDO NATCHITOCHES YATASI ADAI CHOCTAW

"Made in Louisiana" Word Search!

You might be surprised to learn how many things are made, grown, or mined in Louisiana. See if you can find these Louisiana products in the word search below:

Word Bank

COTTON	CHEMICALS
PAPER	SOYBEANS
SUGARCANE	PETROLEUM

P	E	T	R	O	L	E	U	M	X	S	L	K	J	H	P
D	A	Q	Z	M	B	H	N	J	M	N	F	E	G	K	R
K	Q	P	W	C	O	G	T	C	X	V	S	C	A	J	C
Q	Z	W	E	S	U	G	A	R	C	A	N	E	M	D	O
C	C	V	T	R	I	X	O	P	Y	H	T	R	R	F	T
P	L	H	M	T	N	H	N	R	V	F	C	N	X	S	T
A	C	H	E	M	I	C	A	L	S	Y	H	U	J	I	O
P	N	J	X	V	F	G	H	E	M	Y	G	F	X	C	N
E	K	D	W	M	S	N	S	R	F	L	C	I	C	J	C
R	K	W	S	O	Y	B	E	A	N	S	E	L	X	V	H
P	B	G	S	K	C	M	S	K	H	W	R	S	E	K	L

In the Beginning…
Came the Spanish

Hernando de Soto was the first European to explore the area now known as Louisiana. He was looking for gold in the New World. After he was appointed the governor of Cuba, he decided to go exploring. In 1541 and 1542, he led a group of soldiers, slaves, and missionaries through Arkansas and into northern Louisiana.

Help Hernando de Soto find his way to the Mississippi River!

Sing Like a Louisiana Bird Word Jumble

Arrange the jumbled letters in the proper order for the names of birds found in Louisiana.

BLUE JAY
CATBIRD
BOBWHITE
FINCH
BROWN THRASHER
ORIOLE
THRUSH
SPARROW
WARBLER
WOODPECKER

H R T S U H ______________

O O I R L E ______________

T A B C R I D ______________

H C N I F ______________

B W B O T I E H ______________

S P R R W O A ______________

B E U L A J Y __________ ________

B R L W A R E ______________

N W O R B R E H S A R H T __________ ______________

D O O W P C E E K R ______________

Mardi Gras

Every year, New Orleans HOSTS a huge party called "Mardi Gras." This carnival begins 2 weeks before Fat Tuesday. In fact, that's where the festival got its name — "Fat Tuesday" is the English TRANSLATION of "Mardi Gras." During the Mardi Gras PROCESSIONS, people throw beads and other TRINKETS to the crowds. Parades and fancy-dress balls make the city both beautiful and exciting. City clubs SPONSOR the parades, and build incredible floats. People travel from all over the country to be a part of the celebration!

See if you can figure out the meanings of these words from the story above.

1. hosts:____
2. translation:____________________________________
3. processions:___________________________________
4. trinkets:_______________________________________
5. sponsor:_______________________________________

Now check your answers in a dictionary, and see how close you got!

Let's Get Physical!

When we learn about geography, we use special words. These words describe the things that make each part of Louisiana interesting.

See if you can match these geographical terms with their definitions.

1. delta ____
2. bayou ____
3. tributary ____
4. region ____
5. mound ____
6. swamp ____
7. peninsula ____
8. bay ____
9. plain ____
10. levee ____

A. a long piece of land that is surrounded by water on three sides

B. piece of land formed when soil is deposited at the mouth of a river.

C. a pile or heap of earth

D. a part of the sea that cuts into a coastline and forms a shallow curve

E. a bank built along a river to keep it from overflowing

F. a river or stream that flows into a larger body of water

G. an area of land

H. a slow-moving, marshy body of water that often joins a river or lake with a gulf

I. a piece of wet, spongy land

J. a low, flat land area

ANSWERS: 1.B 2.H 3.F 4.G 5.C 6.I 7.A 8.D 9.J 10.E

Louisiana State Flag

Louisiana has had several official flags throughout its history. The current flag is a blue banner, with a picture of a mother pelican in her nest with three young pelicans. The flag also shows the state motto, "Union, Justice, and Confidence." Color the state flag.

Louisiana, The Pelican State!

Match the name of each Louisiana state symbol on the left with its picture on the right.

State Bird

State Flower

State Insect

State Tree

State Amphibian

State Crustacean

State Mammal

Who is a Creole?

People often use the word "Creole" to refer to all people from Louisiana. In fact, the word "creole" is a distortion of the Spanish word "criollo," which means "white child born in the colonies." Creoles were the descendants of the early French and Spanish colonists, while Cajuns' ancestors were Acadian colonists. Historically, Creoles were the wealthy elite upper class in early Louisiana. Today, the Creoles and Cajuns have partially merged together.

Label each statement as either fact (F) or opinion (O)

1. Creoles are much better cooks. _____

2. Cajuns are descendants of Acadian colonists. ____

3. Cajuns talk in an interesting way. _____

4. The word "creole" comes from a Spanish word. _____

5. Creoles were descendants of the Spanish and French colonists. _____

ANSWERS: 1.O 2.F 3.O 4.F 5.F

Places to go! Things to do!

Use the Word Bank to help you complete the sentences below and learn about some of the exciting Louisiana sites you can visit!

1. See historic architecture and listen to jazz music in the ___ ___ ___ ___ ___ ___ Quarter section of New Orleans!

2. Learn about the yellow mineral sulphur at the ___ ___ ___ ___ ___ ___ ___ ___ ___ Museum.

3. Go hunting for Jean Lafitte's treasure on ___ ___ ___ ___ ___ Island.

4. See Army training in progress at Fort ___ ___ ___ ___, near Leesville.

5. Watch out for the alligators while you see beautiful birds at the ___' ___ ___ ___ ___ ___ ___ ___ National Wildlife Refuge.

6. Do you want to learn about pirates? ___ ___ ___ ___ ___ ___ ___ ___ ___ ___ Days in Lake Charles is the perfect event!

7. Do you like Cajun cooking? Go to ___ ___ ___ ___ ___ ___ and be a judge at the World Championship Etouffeé Cookoff!

8. Learn about African-American heritage and history at the ___ ___ ___ ___ ___ ___ ___ Center at Tulane University.

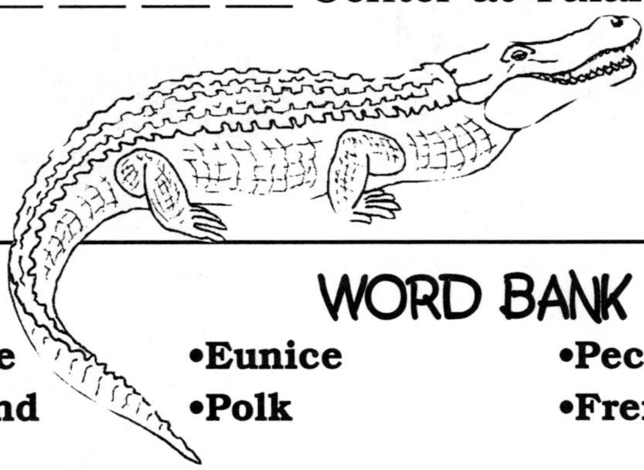

WORD BANK

•D'Arbonne	•Eunice	•Pecan	•Brimstone
•Contraband	•Polk	•French	•Amistad

ANSWERS: 1.French 2.Brimstone 3.Pecan 4.Polk 5.D'Arbonne 6.Contraband 7.Eunice 8.Amistad

Louisiana Plantation

In the 1800s, cotton and sugar cane became important Louisiana crops. Cotton was grown all over the state, and sugar plantations were built in the bayous of southern Louisiana.

Each plantation had a "big house," where the owner and his family lived. There were also smaller buildings. The slaves' quarters, kitchen, and a guest house were often found separate from the big house. Storehouses, stables, and a pigeon house were also on the grounds.

Here is the "big house" of a cotton plantation. Draw in a stable, storehouse, kitchen building, and guest house. Make sure you label them!

Buzzing Around Louisiana!

Write the answers to the questions below. To get to the beehive, follow a path through the maze in the same order as your answers.

1. Louisiana is bordered by the Gulf of ___ ___ ___ ___ ___ ___.
2. Louisiana is the ___ ___th state.
3. The capital of Louisiana is ___ ___ ___ ___ ___ ___ ___ ___ ___ ___.
4. American ___ ___ ___ ___ ___ ___ ___ were the first people to live in Louisiana.
5. There are over 200 ___ ___ ___ ___ domes in Louisiana.
6. ___ ___ ___ ___ ___ ___ ___ ___ Mountain is the highest point in Louisiana.
7. The Cajuns were originally from ___ ___ ___ ___ ___ ___.
8. Jean Lafitte was a ___ ___ ___ ___ ___ ___.
9. Louisiana was sold by ___ ___ ___ ___ ___ ___ ___ ___ to America.
10. René-Robert Cavalier named Louisiana in honor of ___ ___ ___ ___ ___ ___ ___ ___ ___ ___ ___ ___.

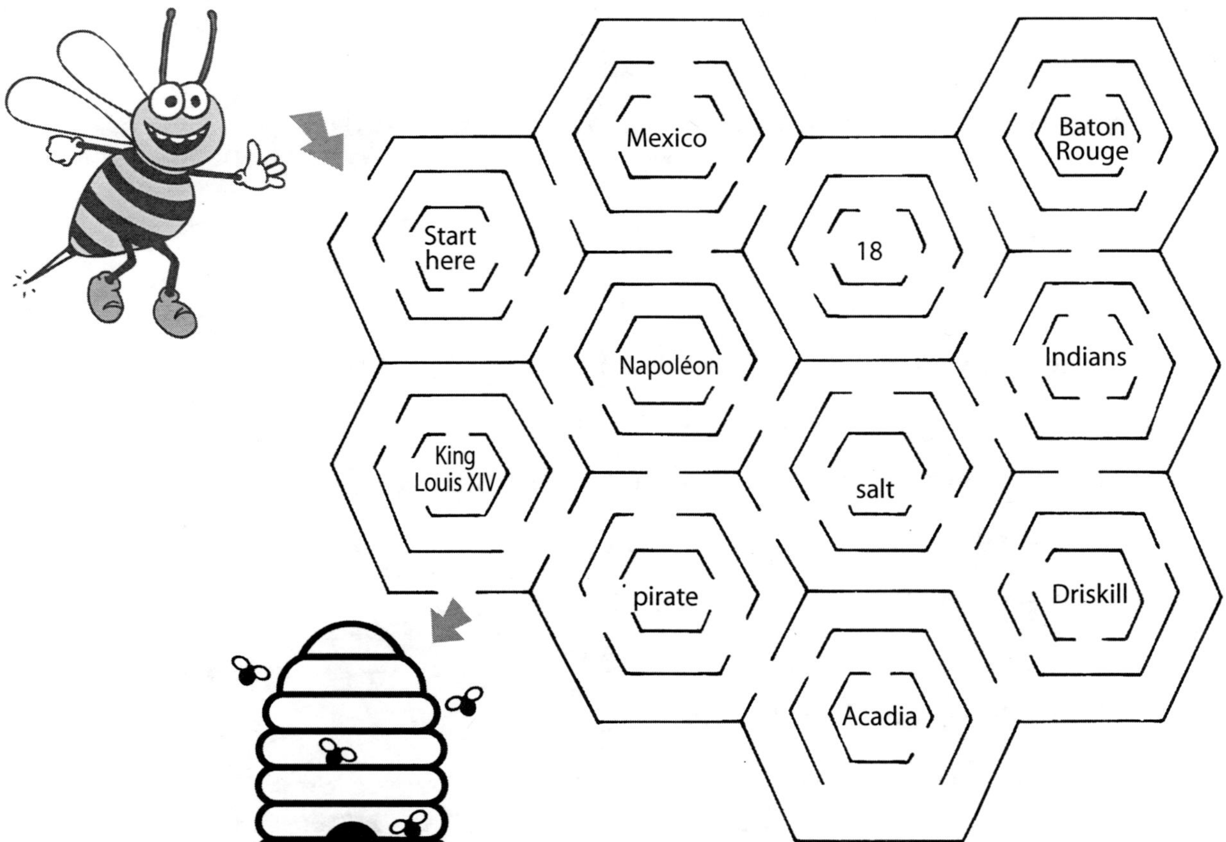

ANSWERS: 1.Mexico 2.18 3.Baton Rouge 4.Indians 5.salt 6.Driskill 7.Acadia 8.pirate 9.Napoléon 10.King Louis XIV

Louisiana Through the Years

Many great things have happened in Louisiana throughout its history. Chronicle the following important Louisiana events by solving math problems to find out the years in which they happened.

1. Hernando de Soto discovers the Mississippi River.

   1x1= 3+2= 2x2= 0+1=

2. La Salle claims Louisiana for France.

   0+1= 3x2= 4+4= 5-3=

3. New Orleans is founded.

   5÷5= 4+3= 9-8= 5+3=

4. Sugar cane is first planted in Louisiana.

   4-3= 5+2= 8-3= 7-6=

5. The United States buys Louisiana from Napoléon.

   2÷2= 2x4= 8-8= 6-3=

6. Louisiana becomes the 18th state.

   5-4= 2+6= 3-2= 2x1=

7. The Battle of New Orleans is won by Andrew Jackson.

   3÷3= 7+1= 8-7= 4+1=

8. Baton Rouge is made the capital of Louisiana.

   6÷6= 4+4= 8÷2= 3x3=

9. Louisiana secedes from the Union.

   2-1= 2x4= 3x2= 6-5=

10. Oil is first discovered in Louisiana.

    9-8= 6+3= 9-9= 7-6=

ANSWERS: 1.1541 2.1682 3.1718 4.1751 5.1803 6.1812 7.1815 8.1849 9.1861 10.1901

Jean Lafitte: Hero or Villain?

Once there was a blacksmith named Jean Lafitte. This blacksmith led a double life, though. He was actually a pirate and a smuggler! He attacked ships in the Gulf of Mexico, stealing their money and cargo. The Louisiana governor knew what Lafitte was doing, but was so busy with the War of 1812 that he couldn't do anything about it.

Lafitte was asked by the British to fight for them against the Americans. Lafitte decided to offer his help to General Andrew Jackson instead. Thanks in part to Lafitte and his pirates, Jackson was able to defeat the British at the Battle of New Orleans. After the war, Lafitte went back to pirating until he left Louisiana in 1819.

Answer the following questions in complete sentences.

1. What was Jean Lafitte's secret?

____

2. Who first asked Lafitte to fight for them?

____

3. Who did Lafitte decide to fight for in the War of 1812?

____

4. What did Lafitte do after the War of 1812?

____

ANSWERS: (may vary slightly) 1.He was a pirate. 2.The British asked Lafitte to fight. 3.The Americans (or Andrew Jackson) received his help. 4.He went back to pirating.

A Louisiana Basketful

Match the name of each crop or product from Louisiana with the basket full of that item.

corn | apples | tomatoes | eggs

crabs and fish | corn, potatoes, onions, and peppers

Louisiana's Venomous Snakes!

Five types of venomous (poisonous) snakes live in Louisiana.

Using the alphabet code, see if you can find out their names.

Use the code to complete the sentences.

A	B	C	D	E	F	G	H	I	J	K	L	M	N	O	P	Q	R	S	T
1	2	3	4	5	6	7	8	9	10	11	12	13	14	15	16	17	18	19	20

U	V	W	X	Y	Z
21	22	23	24	25	26

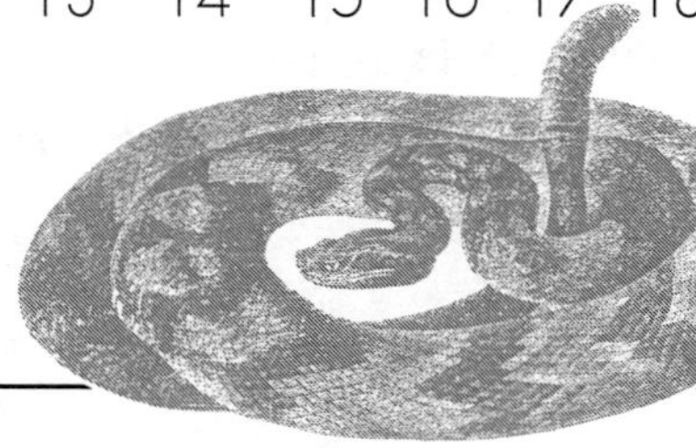

1. ___ ___ ___ ___ ___   ___ ___ ___ ___ ___
3 15 18 1 12   19 14 1 11 5

2. ___ ___ ___ ___ ___ ___ ___   ___ ___ ___ ___ ___
23 5 19 20 5 18 14   16 25 7 13 25
___ ___ ___ ___ ___ ___ ___ ___ ___ ___ ___
18 1 20 20 12 5 19 14 1 11 5

3. ___ ___ ___ ___ ___ ___ ___ ___ ___
3 1 14 5 2 18 5 1 11
___ ___ ___ ___ ___ ___ ___ ___ ___ ___ ___
18 1 20 20 12 5 19 14 1 11 5

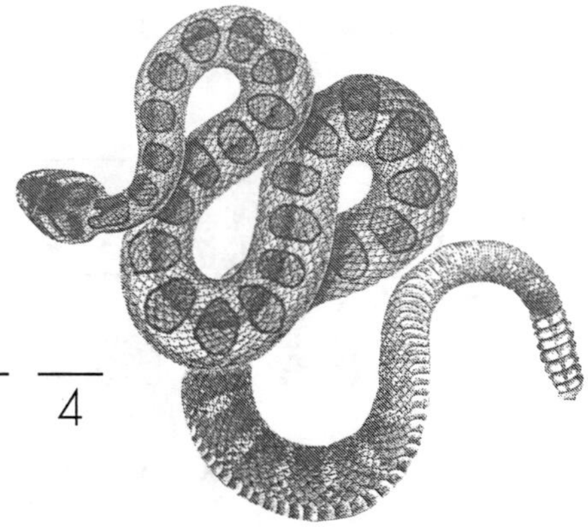

4. ___ ___ ___ ___ ___ ___ ___ ___ ___ ___
3 15 16 16 5 18 8 5 1 4

5. ___ ___ ___ ___ ___   ___ ___ ___ ___ ___ ___ ___ ___
23 1 20 5 18   13 15 3 3 1 19 9 14

ANSWERS: 1.coral snake 2.western pygmy rattlesnake 3.canebrake rattlesnake 4.copperhead 5.water moccasin

Higher Education

The College of Orleans, founded in 1811, was the first college in Louisiana. Louisiana State University first opened in Jackson as the College of Louisiana and then moved to Alexandria in 1860. LSU now has campuses in Alexandria, Eunice, and Shreveport. There are also several private universities in Louisiana, including Tulane and Loyola.

Unscramble the names of these Louisiana schools. Use the Word Bank to help you.

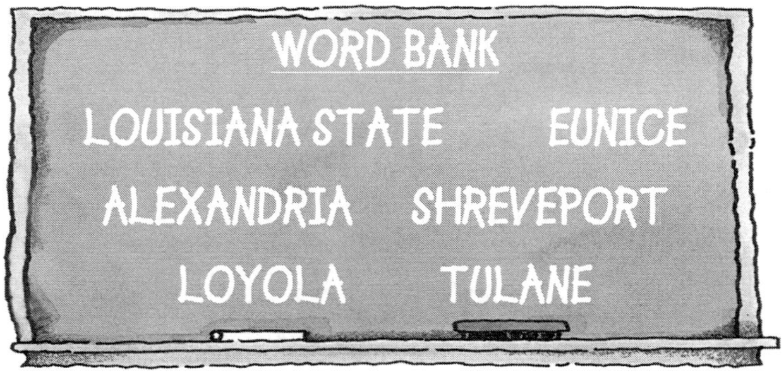

1. R E V R P O H S E T ______________________
2. E N E U I C ______________
3. N L T U E A ______________
4. E X R A D I L N A A ______________________
5. U O I L S A N I A E S T A T ____________ ____________
6. A L O Y L O ___________________

ANSWERS: 1.Shreveport 2.Eunice 3.Tulane 4.Alexandria 5.Louisiana State 6.Loyola

Louisiana Word Wheel

Using the Word Wheel of Louisiana names, answer the following questions.

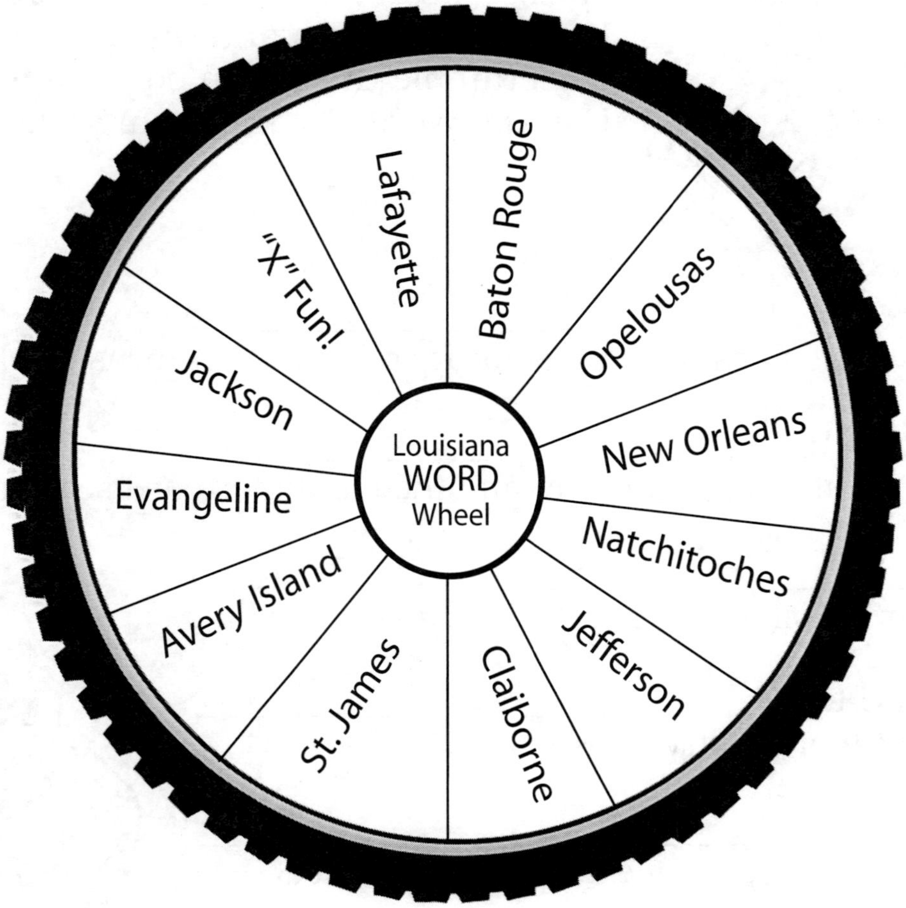

1. The oldest settlement in Louisiana is ____________________________.
2. When Louisiana was under French and Spanish rule, its capital was ___________ ____________________________.
3. Jim Bowie used to live in ____________________________.
4. The Live Oak Society was founded in _______________ by Dr. Edwin L. Stephens.
5. Henry Wadsworth Longfellow wrote a poem about an Acadian refugee named ____________________________.
6. Tabasco sauce is manufactured on _________________ _________________.
7. The first territorial governor of Louisiana was William ___________________.
8. Pecans were first scientifically cultivated in _____________ _____________ Parish.
9. The Louisiana city whose name means "red stick" is ___________ ___________.
10. The Battle of New Orleans was won by General Andrew ___________________.

ANSWERS: 1.Natchitoches 2.New Orleans 3.Opelousas 4.Lafayette 5.Evangeline 6.Avery Island 7.Claiborne 8.St. James 9.Baton Rouge 10.Jackson

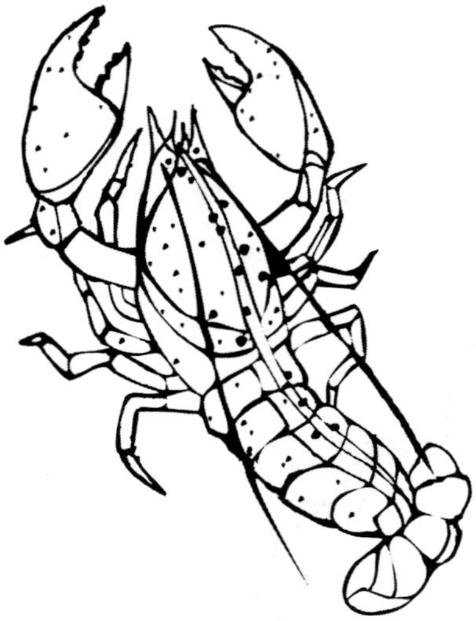

Cajun Cooking

Cajun food is unique. Combinations of spices, meats, and vegetables create tastes that are delicious and distinctively Cajun. Unscramble the Cajun cooking terms below. Use the Word Bank to help you.

1. D E N E B A C L K ______________________
   to fry a season-coated piece of meat or fish until it turns black

2. E S E S A F I R C ______________________
   to cook meat or fowl in butter and then in a thickened seasoned liquid

3. X O R U ______________
   a mixture of oil or butter and flour

4. D R O L A U E ______________________
   rolled meat or poultry

5. L I L R G D E A ______________________
   thinly sliced strips of meat that are pan fried

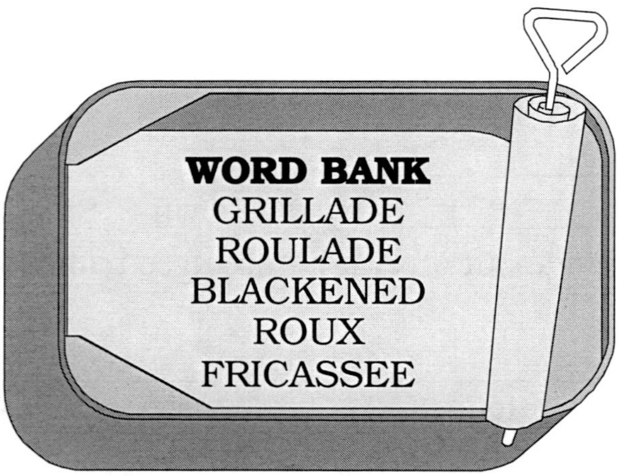

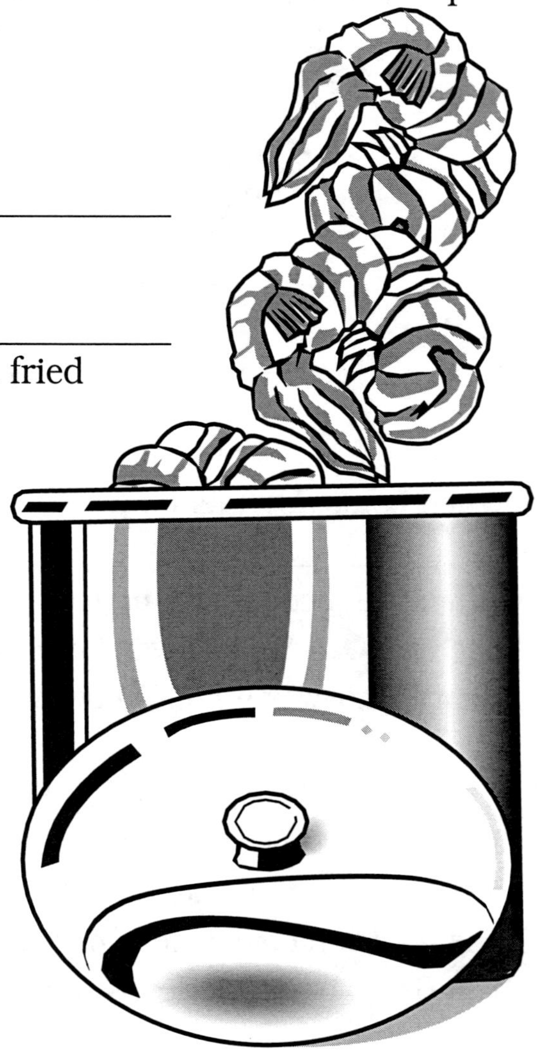

ANSWERS: 1.blackened 2.fricasse 3.roux 4.roulade 5.grillade

Mixed-Up States!

Color, cut out, and paste each of Louisiana's three neighbors onto the map of the Southeast.

Be sure and match the state shapes!

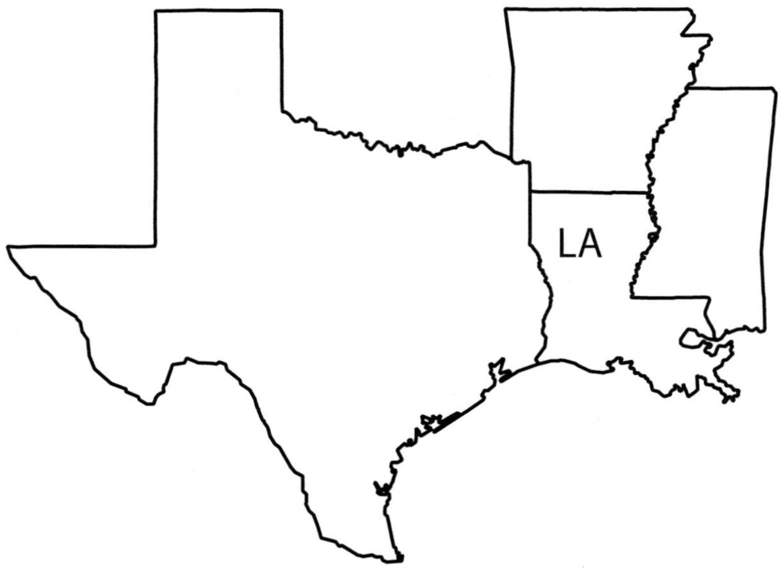

Louisiana Law Comes In Many Flavors!

Here is a matching activity for you to see just a few of the many kinds of law it takes to run our state. See how well you do!

People	**Types of Law:**
1. Bank robber	A. Military Law
2. Business person	B. International Law
3. State park ranger	C Constitutional Law
4. Louisianian	D. Medical Law
5. Hospital	E. Maritime Law
6. Real estate agent	F. Commercial Law
7. Corporate president	G. Criminal Law
8. Ship owner	H. Property Law
9. Diplomat	I. Antitrust Law
10. Soldier	J. Environmental Law

ANSWERS: 1.G 2.F 3.J 4.C 5.D 6.H 7.I 8.E 9.B 10.A

People and Their Jobs!

Can you identify these people and their jobs?

Put an A by the person working on a Louisiana farm.
Put a B by the person working at Fort Polk.
Put a C by the person that works on a boat on the Gulf of Mexico.
Put a D by the New Orleans jazz musician.
Put an E by the person working in a Louisiana salt mine.

Create Your Own Quarter

Look at the change in your pocket. You might notice that one of the coins has changed. The United States is minting new quarters, one for each of the fifty states. Each quarter has a design on it that says something special about one particular state. That means that Louisiana has its very own special quarter design!

What do you think should be on the Louisiana quarter? Draw a picture of how you would like the Louisiana quarter to look. Make sure you include things that are special about Louisiana.

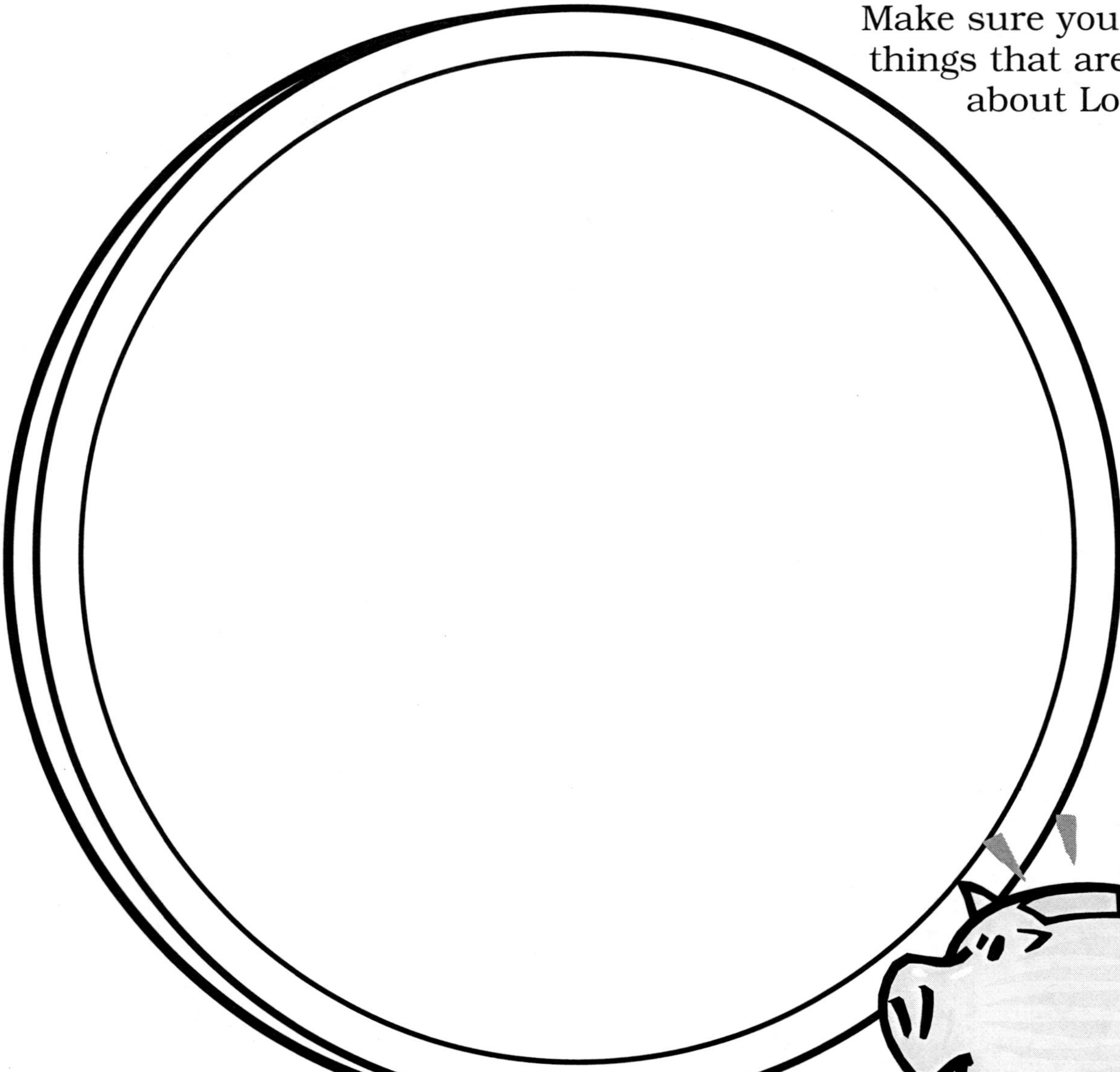

What Shall I Be When I Grow Up?

Here are just a few of the jobs that kept early Louisianans busy.

Lawyer
Judge
Politician
Teacher
Mayor
Carpenter
Gardener
Cook
Laundress
Stablehand
Baker
Fisherman
Crabber
Hunter
Beekeeper

Fur Trader
Housekeeper
Dairyman
Servant
Plantation Owner
Weaver
Mantuamaker (dressmaker)
Musician
Jeweler
Tailor
Pharmacist
Doctor
Milliner (hatmaker)
Blacksmith
Gunsmith

Woodcarver
Silversmith
Wheelwright
Cabinetmaker
Cooper (barrelmaker)
Barber
Printer
Bookbinder
Innkeeper
Minister
Gaoler (jailer)
Governor
Soldier
Sailor
Prospector

You are a young colonist trying to decide what you want to be when you grow up.

Choose a career and next to it write a description of what you think you would do each day as a:

Write your career choice here!

Write your career choice here!

Write your career choice here!

Write your career choice here!

Weather to Please

Louisiana is known for its short mild winters and long, hot, humid summers The highest temperature ever recorded was 114° F (46° C) in 1936, but a typical July will range from the lower 80s F (20s C) to about 95° F (35° C). Summers can sometimes feel hot and humid, but the coastal areas are cooler because of breezes from the Gulf of Mexico.

The coldest Louisiana temperature was recorded in 1899, when it dropped to -16° F (-27° C)! Usually winter temperatures in January are between 0° F (-6° C) and 46° F (8° C). Cold spells rarely last very long.

On the thermometer gauges below, color the mercury red (°F) to show the hottest temperature ever recorded in Louisiana. Color the mercury blue (°F) to show the coldest temperature ever recorded in Louisiana.

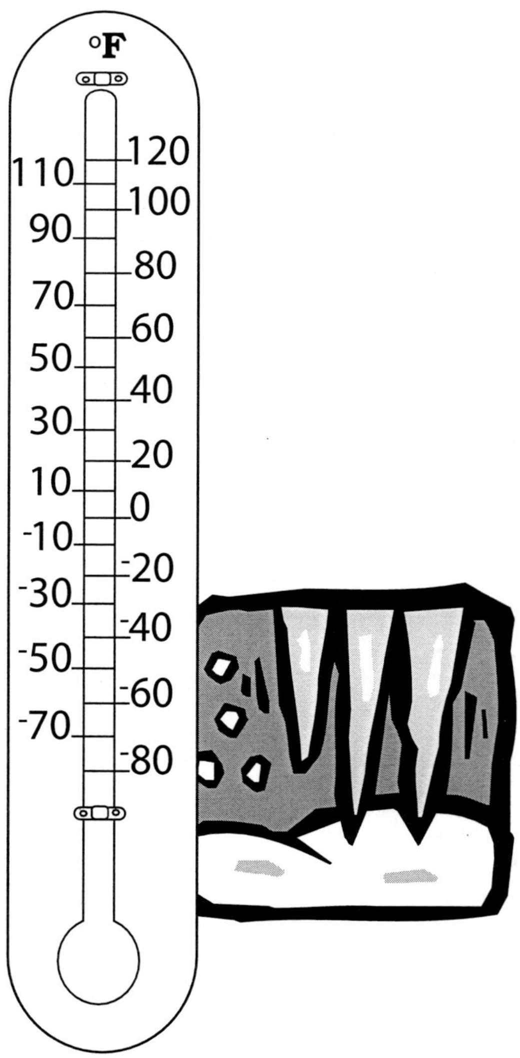

Our State's Governor

The governor is the leader of the state.
Do some research to complete this biography of the governor.

Governor's Name:

____

Paste a picture of the governor here:

The governor was born in this state:

____

The governor was born on this date:

____

Members of the governor's family:

____

____

Interesting facts about the governor:

____

____

____

____

____

____

____

____

Louisiana Indians!

Caddo, Choctaw, Adai, and other Indians were the first people living in Louisiana. They lived in the New World before the explorers and colonists came.

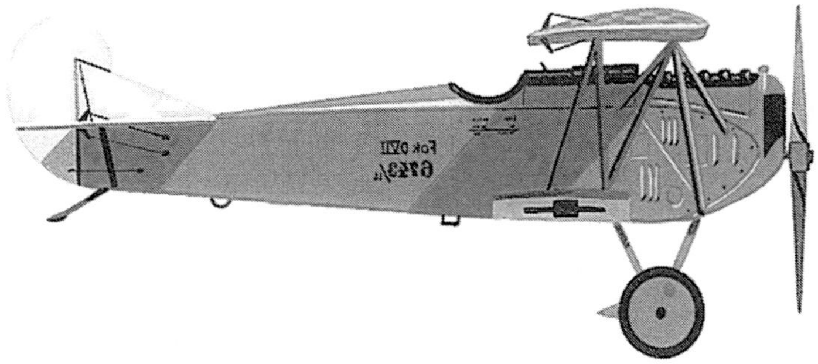

Circle the things that Indians might have used in their everyday life.

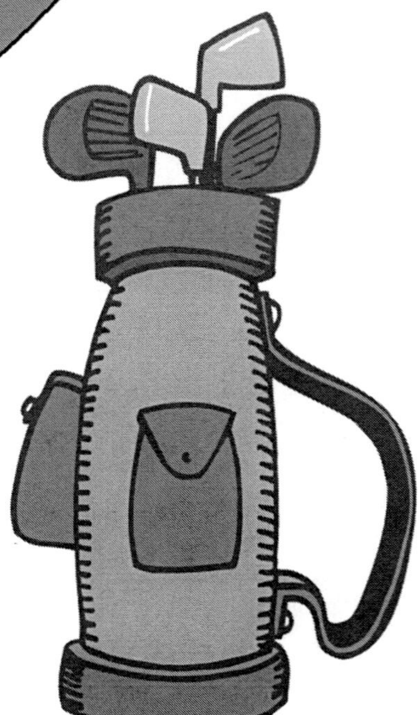

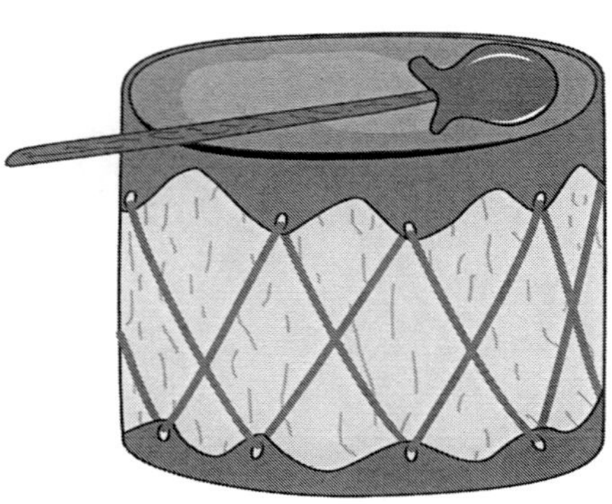

States All Around Code-Buster

Decipher the code and write in the names of the states that border Louisiana.

A	B	C	D	E	F	G	H	I	J	K	L	M	N	O	P	Q	R
✸	❁	✣	♣	➳	❤	❢	✲	✄	✆	☛	✈	✉	✿	✩	✦	✡	✐

S	T	U	V	W	X	Y	Z
❦	☎	✒	✚	✖	✍	✠	✓

1. ___ ___ ___ ___ ___ ___ ___ ___ ___ ___ ___
✉ ✄ ❦ ❦ ✄ ❦ ❦ ✄ ✦ ✦ ✄

2. ___ ___ ___ ___ ___ ___ ___ ___
✸ ✐ ☛ ✸ ✿ ❦ ✸ ❦

3. ___ ___ ___ ___ ___
☎ ➳ ✍ ✸ ❦

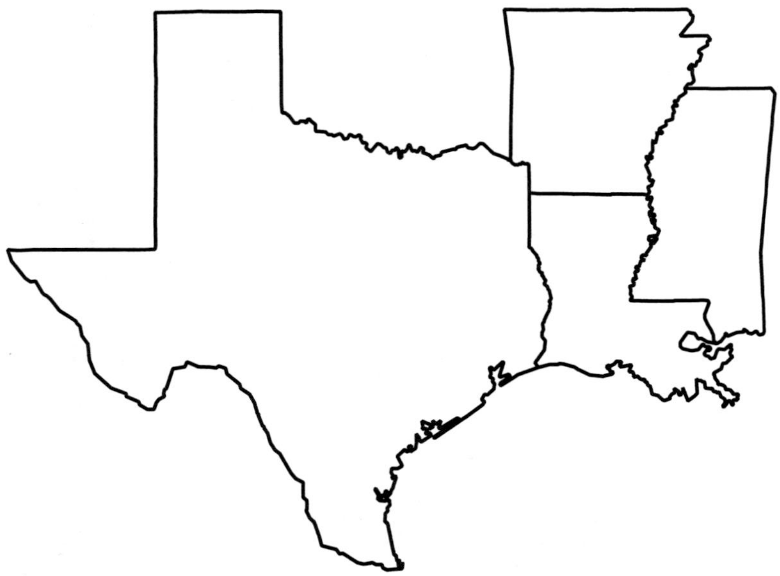

ANSWERS: 1. Mississippi 2. Arkansas 3. Texas

Unique Louisiana Place Names

Can you figure out the compound words that make up the names of these Louisiana cities?

AIMWELL
_______ _______

ASHLAND
_______ _______

BALDWIN
_______ _______

BAYWOOD
_______ _______

BLACKBURN
_______ _______

BURNSIDE
_______ _______

CHATHAM
_______ _______

EASTWOOD
_______ _______

EVERGREEN
_______ _______

FLATWOODS
_______ _______

FRIENDSHIP
_______ _______

GRAYSON
_______ _______

GEORGETOWN
_______ _______

HUTTON
_______ _______

LAKELAND
_______ _______

MIDLAND
_______ _______

NEWLIGHT
_______ _______

RACELAND
_______ _______

Looking For a Home!

Draw a line from the things on the left to their homes on the right!

1. jazz musician	A. D'Arbonne National Wildlife Refuge
2. birds and alligators	B. Driskill Mountain
3. live oaks	C. New Orleans
4. mythical Evangeline	D. Fort Polk
5. Tabasco lover	E. Lafayette
6. United States soldier	F. Avery Island
7. salt miner	G. salt domes
8. mountain climber	H. Baton Rouge
9. Louisiana's governor	I. Opelousas
10. Jim Bowie	J. St. Martinville

ANSWERS: 1.C 2.A 3.E 4.J 5.F 6.D 7.G 8.B 9.H 10.I

Louisiana-Chat

Both Cajuns and Creoles can trace their roots back to French ancestors. They've preserved their French ancestry in many ways, including some of their unique words and phrases.

Here are just a few. See if you can match the Cajun words on the left with their meanings on the right.

1. bayou ____
2. dose ____
3. cher ____
4. dat ____
5. fais-do-do ____
6. rue ____
7. lagniappe ____
8. where y'at ____
9. boucherie ____
10. dey ____

A. dear

B. canal-sized waterway used for boat transportation and fishing

C. that

D. a little extra something for nothing

E. they

F. those

G. a Cajun party in the streets

H. how are you

I. traditional Cajun party

J. street

ANSWERS: 1.B 2.F 3.A 4.C 5.G 6.J 7.D 8.H 9.I 10.E

Something Fishy Here!

Louisiana is filled with waterways. There are bayous, lakes, rivers, swamps, and even the Gulf of Mexico! All sorts of creatures live in these waters, from fish to birds to even alligators. Be sure to watch your step!

Draw what is going on above the water line, and add some other underwater fish friends.

The Scenic Route

Imagine you are the official tour guide for your class and you're taking them on a trip to some famous Louisiana places.
Circle these sites and cities on the map below and then number them in the order you would visit if you were traveling north to south through the state.

_____Lake Pontchartrain
_____Baton Rouge
_____Shreveport
_____Opelousas
_____Alexandria
_____New Orleans
_____Gulf of Mexico
_____Chitimacha Reservation

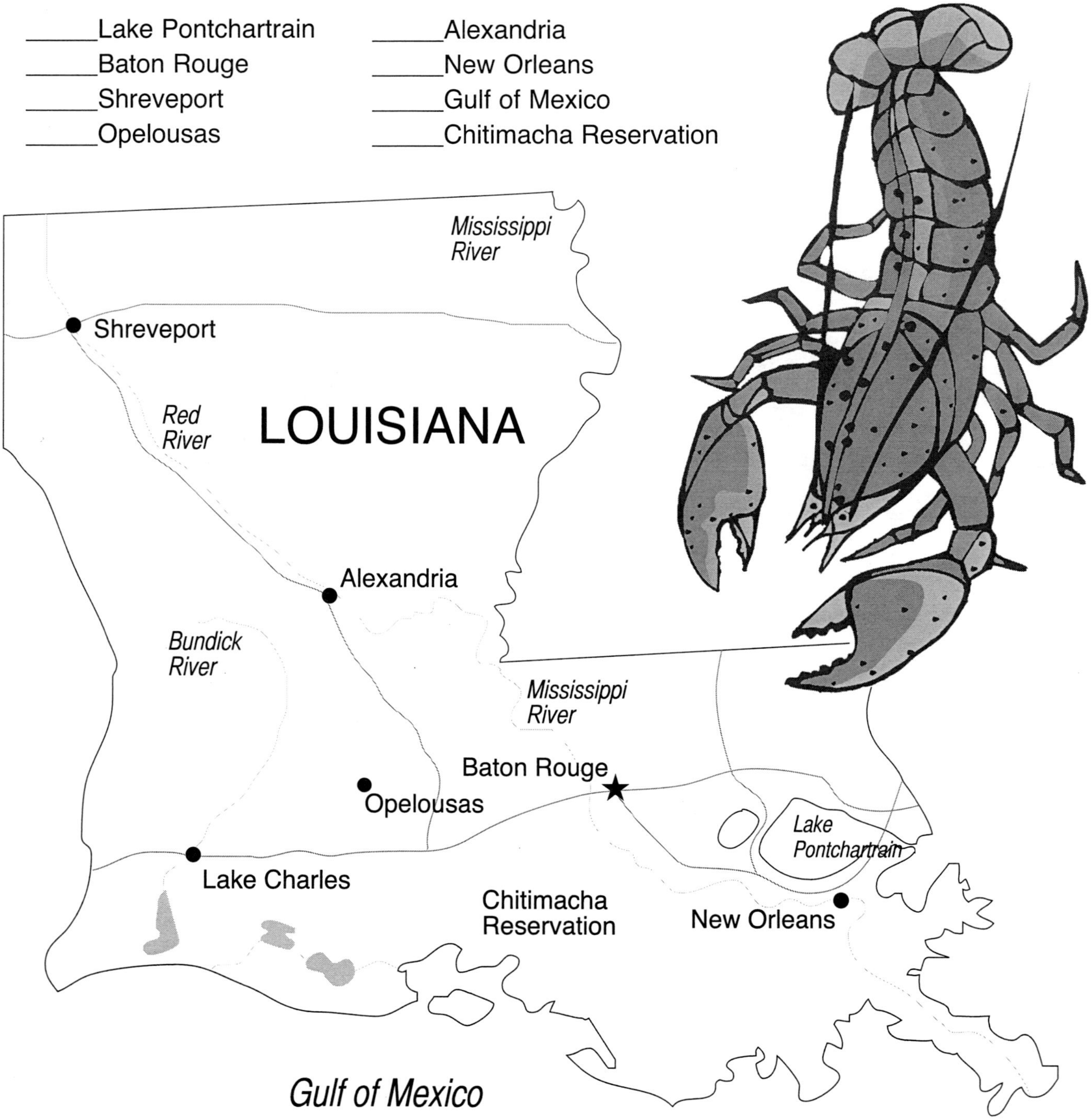

ANSWERS: 1.Shreveport 2.Alexandria 3.Opelousas 4.Baton Rouge 5.Lake Pontchartrain 6.New Orleans 7.Chitimacha Reservation 8.Gulf of Mexico

Key to a Map!

A map key, also called a map legend, shows symbols which represent different things on a map.

Match each word with a symbol for things found in the state of Louisiana.

airport

church

mountains

railroad

river

road

school

state capital

battle site

bird sanctuary

The Ports of Louisiana

Louisiana sits in an ideal location for transportation over water. The Mississippi and several other rivers terminate in the Gulf of Mexico along the southern border of Louisiana. Deep channels in the rivers allow ships to pass through into the Gulf. The South Louisiana port in New Orleans is one of the major ports in the nation. More than 2,500 vessels and 100,000 barges pass through the port every year. Baton Rouge is a major inland port on the Mississippi River. Ships and shipbuilding are an important part of Louisiana life.

When you're on board a ship, you have to use special terms to talk about directions. Label the boats below with these terms:

bow: front of the ship
stern: back of the ship
fore: towards the bow
aft: towards the stern
port: left as you face the bow
starboard: right as you face the bow

___ ___ ___ ___ ___ ___ ___ ___ ___

___ ___ ___ ___ ___

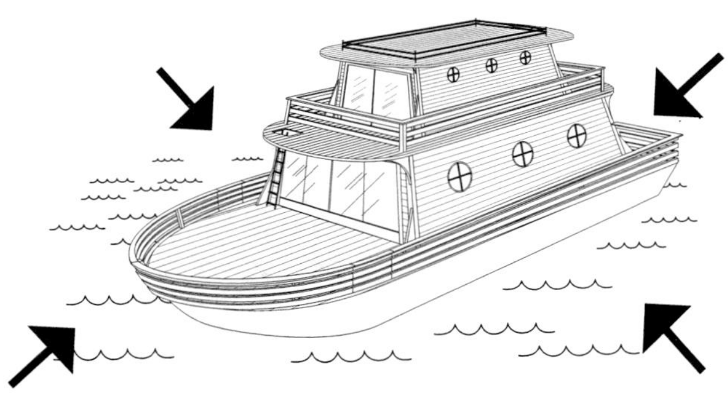

___ ___ ___

___ ___ ___ ___

this arrow is pointing ___ ___ ___ ___

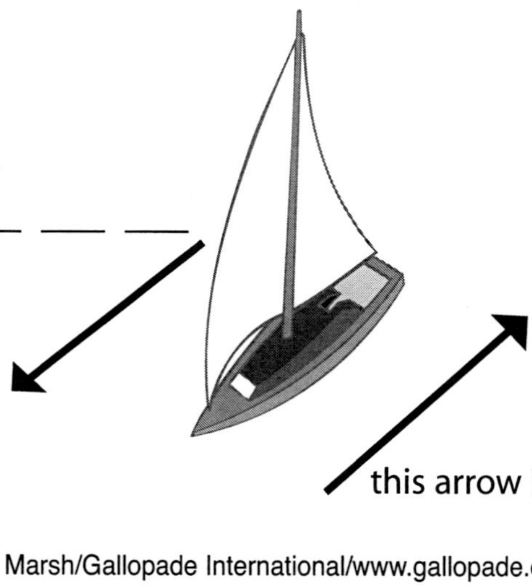

this arrow is pointing ___ ___ ___

Louisiana IMMIGRATION

People have come to Louisiana from many other states and countries. As time has gone by, Louisiana's population has grown more diverse. This means that people of different races and from different cultures and ethnic backgrounds have moved to Louisiana.

In the past, people came to Louisiana from France, Spain, England, Germany, Ireland, and Italy. They also came from Acadia (French Canada) and the West Indies. Slaves migrated (involuntarily) from Africa. People have also come from Asian countries, and just about everywhere else. Only a certain number of immigrants are allowed to move to America each year. Many will become U.S. Citizens.

Read the statement and decide if it's fact or opinion. Write your answer on the line.

1. Many of Louisiana's early immigrants came from Europe. ____________________
2. Lots of immigrants speak a language other than English. ____________________
3. The clothing immigrants wear is very interesting. ____________________
4. Immigrants from England have a neat accent when they speak. ____________________
5. Many immigrants will become United States citizens. ____________________
6. Immigrants love Louisiana's southern cooking. ____________________

ANSWERS: 1.Fact 2.Fact 3.Opinion 4.Opinion 5.Fact 6.Opinion 7.Fact

Home Sweet Home

Many artists, musicians, and writers were either born in Louisiana, or made their homes there.

See if you can match these creative people with their native or adopted hometowns. (New Orleans may be used more than once.)

A. New Orleans; B. Shreveport; C. Opelousas; D. Haynesville

____ 1. Louis Armstrong: jazz trumpeter

____ 2. Geoffrey Beene: fashion designer

____ 3. Van Cliburn: concert pianist

____ 4. Paul Prudhomme: Cajun and Creole chef

____ 5. Lillian Hellman: playwright, wrote *The Children's Hour*

____ 6. John James Audubon: famous for his paintings of birds, wrote *Birds of North America*

____ 7. Truman Capote: novelist, wrote *Breakfast at Tiffanys*

____ 8. George Washington Cable: historian, known for his Creole histories

ANSWERS: 1.A 2.D 3.B 4.C 5.A 6.A 7.A 8.A

Louisiana Women and the Vote!

Until 1920, women were unable to vote in the United States. Then enough states ratified the 19th Amendment to the Constitution, and it became the law of the land. Women gained suffrage nationally, and are still a major force in the election process.

Match the words in the left box with their definitions in the right box.

1. Amendment ______
2. Ratify ______
3. Constitution ______
4. State Senate and House of Representatives ______
5. Law of the Land ______
6. Election ______
7. Suffrage ______
8. Women ______

A. The right to vote

B. A law that is an acceptable practice throughout the nation

C. People who could not vote in Louisiana until 1920

D. An addition to the Constitution

E. The selection, by vote, of a candidate for office

F. To give approval

G. The fundamental law of the United States that was framed in 1787 and put into effect in 1789

H. The legislature in some states of the United States

ANSWERS: 1.D 2.F 3.G 4.H 5.B 6.E 7.A 8.C

Natural Resources

Fill in the bubblegram with some of Louisiana's natural resources. Use the first and last letter clues to help you.

1. P ___ ___ ___ ___ ◯

2. ◯ ___ ___ ___ ___ ___ ___ ___ ◯ S

3. ◯ ___ ___ ◯ ___ E

4. F ___ ◯

5. F ◯ ___ ___

6. C ◯ ___ ___ ___ ◯

7. S ◯ ___ ___ ___ ___ ◯ ___

8. ___ ◯ ___ T

WORD BANK
CATTLE
COTTON
VEGETABLES
FUR
PECANS
FISH
SALT
SOYBEANS

Now unscramble the "bubble" letters to find out the mystery word!
HINT: What is one way we can help to save our environment?

___ ___ ___ ___ ___ ___ ___ ___ ___ ___ ___ ___

MYSTERY WORD: CONSERVATION
ANSWERS: 1.PECANS 2.VEGETABLES 3.CATTLE 4.FUR 5.FISH 6.COTTON 7.SOYBEANS 8.SALT

Louisiana Word Search

Find these Louisiana words in the puzzle below.

WORD BANK

•PARISH •CAJUN •CHER •CREOLE
•GRIS GRIS •RUE •ZYDECO •VOODOO

P	A	R	I	S	H	M	X	T	N	K	C	B	R
X	N	B	L	I	N	K	C	S	R	L	H	N	U
T	E	T	V	I	K	A	K	R	L	N	E	K	E
H	R	B	C	M	F	R	N	E	E	T	R	R	I
E	L	S	M	A	C	N	G	L	K	O	D	F	C
K	I	C	V	O	O	D	O	O	S	X	L	G	X
S	N	T	X	P	C	A	J	U	N	N	C	E	N
K	D	C	I	J	C	X	B	N	I	T	M	I	V
B	L	E	C	O	S	H	O	C	T	O	N	I	O
G	R	I	S	G	R	I	S	D	B	Y	T	O	G
C	Z	Y	D	E	C	O	A	N	X	U	L	S	C

What a Great Idea!

Here are just a few of the wonderful Louisiana inventions, products, and companies.

WORD BANK

• Tabasco • pecans • blues
• sugar • teddy bear

1. President Theodore Roosevelt visited Louisiana in 1902, where he refused to shoot a bear cub. The cartoon that showed the event inspired the creation of the ___ ___ ___ ___ ___ ___ ___ ___ ___.

2. Louisiana is the home of ___ ___ ___ ___ ___ music. Father of the blues, Huddie "Leadbelly" Ledbetter, is buried in Mooringsport.

3. Avery Island is the home of the world famous ___ ___ ___ ___ ___ ___ ___ hot sauce.

4. Jean Étienne Boré was the first to granulate ___ ___ ___ ___ ___.

5. The first recorded scientific cultivation of ___ ___ ___ ___ ___ ___ was in 1846 in St. James Parish.

ANSWERS: 1.teddy bear 2.blues 3.tabasco 4.sugar 5.pecans

Famous Louisiana People Scavenger Hunt

Here is a list of some of the famous people associated with our state. Go on a scavenger hunt to see if you can "capture" a fact about each one. Use an encyclopedia, almanac, or other resource you might need. Happy hunting!

FAMOUS PERSON	FAMOUS FACT
Louis Armstrong	
John James Audubon	
Judah Philip Benjamin	
Jean Étienne Boré	
Truman Capote	
William C.C. Claiborne	
Louis Moreau Gottschalk	
Lillian Hellman	
Mahalia Jackson	
Grace Elizabeth King	
Jean Lafitte	
Huddie "Leadbelly" Ledbetter	
Huey Pierce Long	
John McDonogh	
Troy Houston Middleton	
Leonidas K. Polk	
Paul Prudhomme	
Henry Hobson Richardson	
Edgar Bloom Stern	
Edward Douglass White	

Louisiana Folklore

Use the words in the Word Bank to fill in the blanks in this Louisiana folktale. Some may be used more than once.

Why the Crow is Black

Long ago, the ___ ___ ___ ___ ___ ___ ___ and the crow were the same dull, boring gray. They decided one day that they would ___ ___ ___ ___ ___ each other's ___ ___ ___ ___ ___ ___ ___ ___. So they went out and found many different colors of ___ ___ ___ ___ ___. The ___ ___ ___ ___ ___ ___ ___ asked if the crow would paint his ___ ___ ___ ___ ___ ___ ___ ___ first. The crow painted the ___ ___ ___ ___ ___ ___ ___ with red, blue, yellow, purple, and every other color in the rainbow.

When the crow was done, the ___ ___ ___ ___ ___ ___ ___ saw how ___ ___ ___ ___ ___ ___ ___ ___ ___ he was. He wanted to run out and show his new colors to the world. He didn't want to ___ ___ ___ ___ ___ the crow. So he took a pot of black ___ ___ ___ ___ ___, and threw it at the crow. The ___ ___ ___ ___ ___ soaked into the crow's feathers, making him black as night. Then the ___ ___ ___ ___ ___ ___ ___ ran away laughing.

And that's why the crow is black!

WORD BANK

• peacock • paint • feathers • beautiful

Industrious Louisiana

Louisiana is home to a wide variety of industries. Its location on the Gulf of Mexico makes it an ideal place for shipbuilding, seafood, and transportation industries. Manufacturing, mining, and farming are also important aspects of Louisiana's economy.

For each industry below, write down at least one way it may affect your everyday life.

petroleum:____

____

____

natural gas:____

____

____

agriculture:____

____

____

ports:____

____

____

tourism:____

____

____

fishing:____

____

____

Where Y'at?

Color the state of Louisiana. What color? Why, the state colors of gold, white, and blue, of course! Circle the state capital.

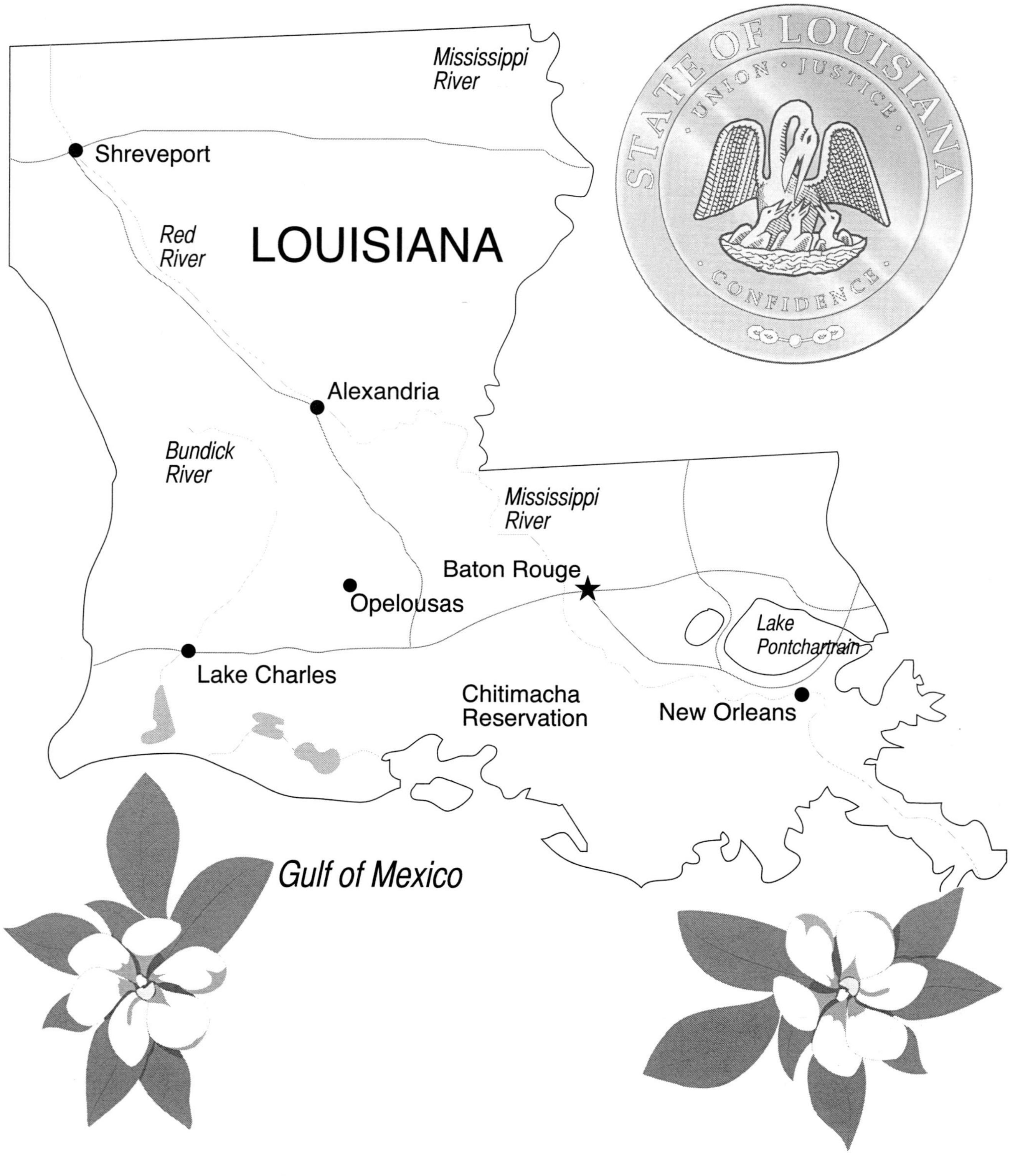

State Greats

How many state greats from Louisiana do you know? Use an encyclopedia, almanac, or other resource to match the following facts with the state great they describe.

1. first elected woman senator in Louisiana
2. governor of Louisiana known as the Kingfish
3. lawyer who fought for civil rights
4. first president of Southwest Louisiana University
5. supported social causes and women's issues
6. first woman to run for governor
7. supported education and had a "Share the Wealth" campaign
8. pushed for construction of a paved highway system
9. was the registrar of the State Land Office in 1952
10. helped desegregate schools in New Orleans
11. started the Live Oak Society
12. was governor of Louisiana in 1920

A. Huey P. Long

B. Alexander Pierre Tureaud

C. Edwin Stevens

D. Lucille May Grace

E. Mary Landrieu

F. John M. Parker

ANSWERS: 1.E 2.A 3.B 4.C 5.E 6.D 7.A 8.F 9.D 10.B 11.C 12.F

Louisiana Writers

Fill in the missing first or last name of these famous Louisiana writers.

1. First name: Truman
   Last name:________________________

2. First name: ________________________
   Last name: Bradford

3. First name: Lyle
   Last name:________________________

4. First name:________________________
   Last name: Cable

5. First name: Lillian
   Last name:________________________

6. First name:________________________
   Last name: King

ANSWERS: 1.Capote 2.Roark 3.Saxon 4.George Washington 5.Hellman 6.Grace Elizabeth

Virtual Louisiana!

Using your knowledge of Louisiana, make a website that explains different places in Louisiana. You can even draw pictures of animals, places, people, and other fun stuff to make your very own interesting website.

Yellow Fever

In the 1800s and early 1900s, Louisianians faced the dreaded disease, yellow fever. Thousands of people were killed every year by this illness. At that time, nobody realized that mosquitos were carriers of the disease. People who were bitten by infected mosquitos often became sick.

Luckily, a Cuban physician figured it out. Dr. Carlos Finlay studied yellow fever and discovered that mosquitos were giving the disease to people. In 1905, Dr. Quitman Kohnke started a program to put screens over the cisterns under New Orleans. Since the mosquitoes couldn't get into the sewer system to breed, they also stopped making people sick. New Orleans has not had a yellow fever problem since then.

SWAT THE SKEETER!
"Swat" the mosquitos by crossing out the letters they're sitting on. Find out the mystery words!

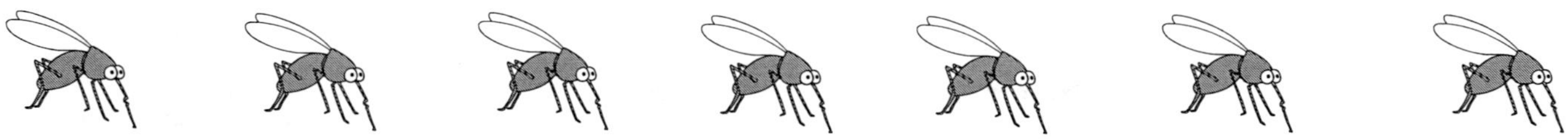

M Y X E V L P L K O M W N

G F L E A V U E Q R S

ANSWERS: yellow fever

A River Runs Through It!

The state of Louisiana is blessed with many rivers.
See if you can wade right in and figure out which river name completes the sentences below!

RIVER BANK
Mississippi Atchafalaya Black
Red Dugdemona

1. Old Man River, the great ___ ___ ___ ___ ___ ___ ___ ___ ___ ___ ___ flows through Louisiana to the Gulf of Mexico.

2. Its name may sound like a sneeze, but the ___ ___ ___ ___ ___ ___ ___ ___ ___ ___ ___ River is quite beautiful.

3. The ___ ___ ___ ___ ___ River is not as dark as it may sound.

4. Another river with an interesting name is the ___ ___ ___ ___ ___ ___ ___ ___ ___ River.

5. I wonder if the ___ ___ ___ river was named for a crawfish boil?

ANSWERS: **1.** Mississippi 2. Atchafalaya 3. black 4. Dugdemona 5. red

Louisiana Trivia

New Orleans is one of the leading cities to consume high quantities of grits.

At Poverty Point, there is a bird-shaped earth mound that is over 3,000 years old and stands over 70 feet (21 meters) tall!

Governor Earl Long was forcibly kidnapped and sent to a mental institution in 1959. Four weeks later, he was back in office and fired the people who sent him there!

The Battle of New Orleans actually took place after the War of 1812 was already over! News of the Treaty of Ghent hadn't reached either General Jackson or the British soldiers when they fought.

Van Cliburn of Shreveport was the first American to win the Tchaikovsky piano competition in 1954.

The first movie filmed in Louisiana was *Faust* in 1908.

The Port of New Orleans has 22 miles (35 kilometers) of loading and unloading facilities, and is the world's longest continuous cargo complex.

Louisiana has had at least 10 official flags. This is more than many other states in the Union.

New Orleans is sinking. The ground the city was built on is actually settling at a rate of 2 inches (8 centimeters) every 100 years!

Plant a Tree

In the late 1800s and early 1900s, railroads altered Louisiana's appearance. Lumber companies took advantage of the transportation. They started cutting down the cypress and pine forests in Louisiana. This devastated huge sections of forest. Sometimes the companies would donate the land to parishes to make up for not paying their taxes.

Between 1940 and 1990, about 5 million acres (2 million hectares) of land were reforested. People have planted trees to try to restore the natural environments destroyed by the lumbering. Today, Louisiana's Department of Agriculture and Forestry is considered one of the best in the nation.

Use the information above to complete the crossword.

1. The lumber companies ____________ huge sections of forest. (ACROSS)
2. People have planted trees in order to ____________ the natural environments. (DOWN)
3. The railroads____________Louisiana's appearance. (DOWN)
4. By 1990, about 5 million acres (2 million hectares) of land were __________. (ACROSS)
5. The lumber companies would sometimes ________ deforested land to the parishes instead of paying their taxes. (ACROSS)

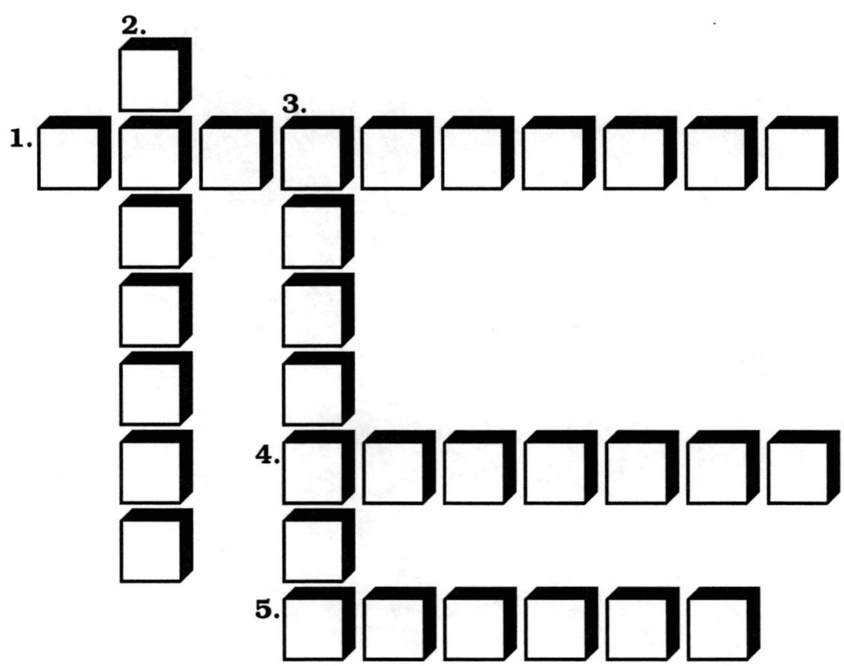

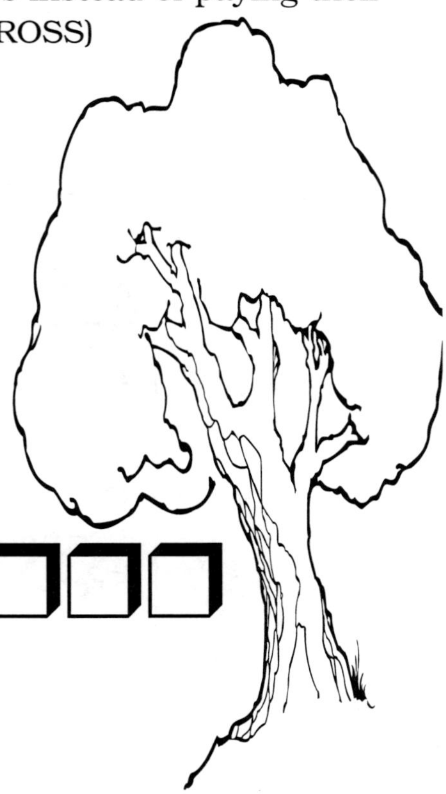

ANSWERS: 1.devastated 2.restore 3.altered 4.reforested 5.donate

Louisiana Gazetteer

A gazetteer is a list of places. Use the word bank to complete the names of some of these famous places in our state:

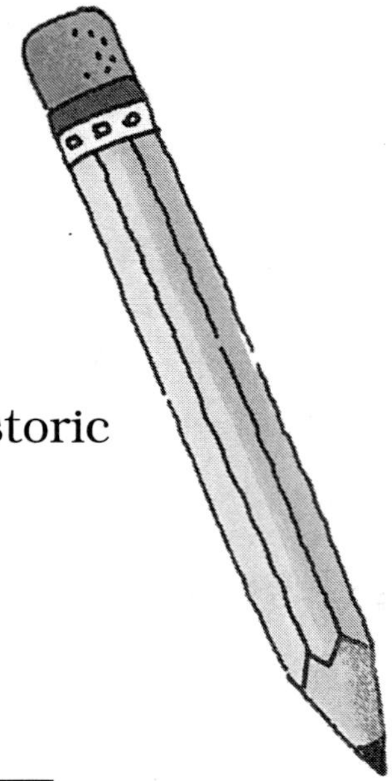

1. The ___ ___ ___ ___ ___ ___ Quarter in New Orleans
2. ___ ___ ___ ___ ___ ___ ___ ___ ___ National Forest
3. ___ ___ ___ ___ ___ ___ ___ ___ Plantation and its historic gardens in St. Francisville
4. The statue of ___ ___ ___ ___ ___ ___ ___ ___ ___ ___ behind St. Martin of Tours Church
5. The Louisiana State ___ ___ ___ ___ ___ ___ ___ ___ ___ near Ville Platte
6. The new capitol building in ___ ___ ___ ___ ___ ___ ___ ___ ___ ___
7. ___ ___ ___ ___ ___ ___ ___ ___ Mountain, the highest point in Louisiana
8. Louisiana's oldest settlement in

   ___ ___ ___ ___ ___ ___ ___ ___ ___ ___ ___ ___

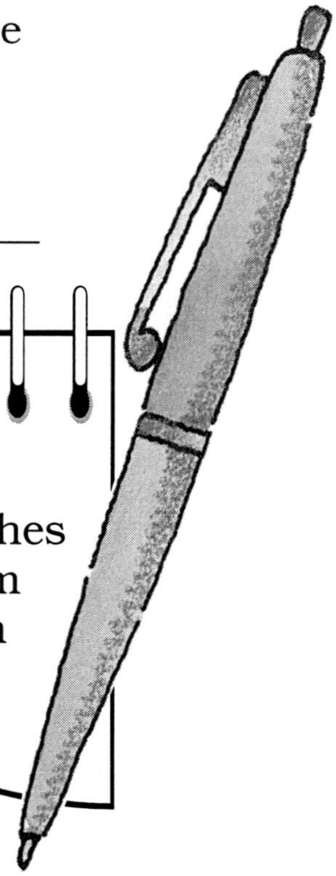

WORD BANK

Driskill	Natchitoches
Evangeline	Arboretum
French	Rosedown
Baton Rouge	Kisatchie

ANSWERS: 1.French 2.Kisatchie 3.Rosedown 4.Evangeline 5.Arboretum 6.Baton Rouge 7.Driskill 8.Natchitoches

State Stuff Jumbles

Unscramble the words below to get the scoop on all the state symbols of Louisiana.

S E A R E T N R W O B N E L I P C N A	______________	STATE BIRD
O I L A G M N A	______________	STATE FLOWER
S E R P S Y C	______________	STATE TREE
T C A A H U O L A E L O A P R D G D O	______________	STATE DOG
S I F C W H R A	______________	STATE CRUSTACEAN
E N E G R R E E T R O F G	______________	STATE AMPHIBIAN
E B E Y N O H E	______________	STATE INSECT
G A L I T R O L A	______________	STATE REPTILE

ANSWERS: 1. eastern brown pelican 2.magnolia 3.cypress 4.catahoula leopard dog 5.crawfish 6.green tree frog 7.honeybee 8.alligator

The Crusty Crustacean

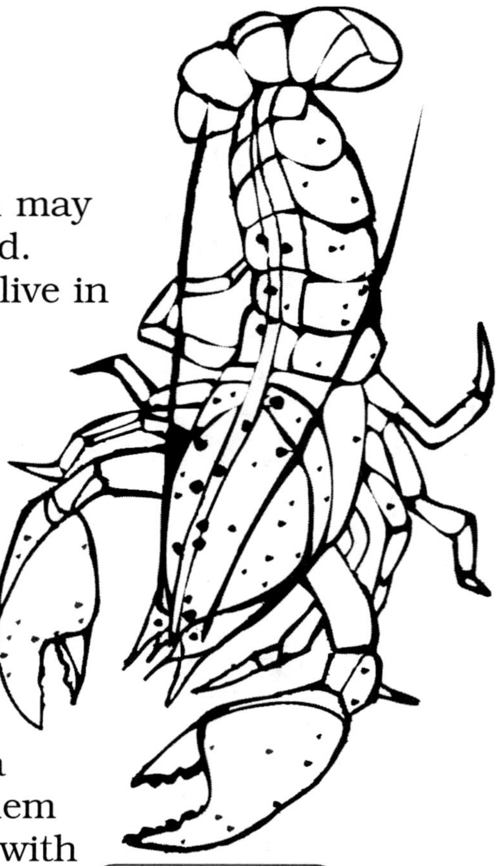

Louisiana has a state crustacean. You may know it as the crawfish, crayfish, or crawdad. These animals look like small lobsters, and live in the lakes, ponds, rivers, and streams of Louisiana. You might also find them in swampy places and wet meadows. Sometimes they live in burrows in the mud. They are freshwater animals, which means that they don't live in the sea. Crayfish are nocturnal. They sleep during the day and then come out at night to feed. Crayfish will eat just about anything, especially plants. Crayfish don't have a skeleton inside them like you do. Instead, a hard shell protects their bodies and gives them shape. They're yummy when they're boiled with Cajun spices!

Answer the following questions:

1. What does "freshwater" mean?______________________________

2. When do crayfish sleep?______________________________

3. What do crayfish eat?______________________________

4. What's your favorite crayfish recipe?______________________________

ANSWERS: (may vary slightly) 1.living in streams or rivers, not the ocean 2.during the day 3.anything, but especially plants 4.will vary

Timeline

A timeline is a list of important events and the year that they happened. You can use a timeline to understand more about history. Read the timeline about Louisiana's history and see if you can answer the questions at the bottom.

A timeline is a list of important events and the year that they happened. You can use a timeline to understand more about history. Read the timeline about Louisiana's history and see if you can answer the questions at the bottom.

1718......................New Orleans is founded and named for the Duc d'Orléans.
1764......................Acadian immigrants arrive from Canada.
1800......................Spain gives Louisiana back to France in the Treaty of San Ildefonso.
1812......................Louisiana becomes the 18th state.
1815......................Andrew Jackson wins the Battle of New Orleans.
1849......................Baton Rouge becomes the capital of Louisiana.
1861......................Louisiana secedes from the Union.
1901......................Oil is first discovered in Louisiana.
1927......................The worst flood in U.S. history leaves 300,000 people homeless.
1984......................Louisiana's World Fair is held in New Orleans.

Now put yourself back in the proper year if you were the following people.

1. If you are amazed to hear that oil has been found in Louisiana, the year would be ____________.
2. If you are happy to hear that General Jackson defeated the British in New Orleans, the year would be______________.
3. If you are an Acadian immigrant nervous about arriving at your new home, the year would be______________.
4. If you are horrified to hear that a flood has destroyed hundreds of thousands of homes, the year would be____________.
5. If you are a Spaniard disappointed that your country had to give Louisiana back to France, the year would be____________.

ANSWER: 1.1901 2.1815 3.1764 4.1927 5.1800

Louisiana Banks

Louisiana banks provide essential financial services.
Some of the services that banks provide include:

* They lend money to consumers to purchase goods and services such as houses, cars, and education.
* They lend money to producers who start new businesses.
* They issue credit cards.
* They provide savings accounts and pay interest to savers.
* They provide checking accounts.

Circle whether you would have more, less, or the same amount of money after each event.

1. You deposit your paycheck into your checking account.	MORE	LESS	SAME
2. You put $1,000 in your savings account.	MORE	LESS	SAME
3. You use your credit card to buy new school clothes.	MORE	LESS	SAME
4. You borrow money from the bank to open a toy store.	MORE	LESS	SAME
5. You write a check at the grocery store.	MORE	LESS	SAME
6. You transfer money from checking to savings.	MORE	LESS	SAME

ANSWERS: 1.more 2.more 3.less 4.more 5.less 6.same

I Am A Famous Person From Louisiana

From the Word Bank, find my name and fill in the blank. (My name might be used twice.)

WORD BANK

Louis Armstrong	Lillian Hellman
Huey Long	Evangeline
Dolores Spike	William Claiborne

1. I am a playwright from New Orleans. I became internationally known for my plays *The Children's Hour* and *The Little Foxes.*

Who am I? ____________________ ______________________

2. I was the first African-American woman to head a major liberal-arts college. I was the chancellor of Southern University.

Who am I? ____________________ ______________________

3. I am a fictional character in one of Henry Wadsworth Longfellow's poems. I was an Acadian refugee who lost and found my love.

Who am I? ____

4. I was the first territorial governor of Louisiana. I had a lot of responsibility, and was ordered to take over West Florida.

Who am I? ____________________ ______________________

5. I was a famous jazz trumpeter. I lived in New Orleans and loved to play my music there.

Who am I? ____________________ ______________________

6. I was the governor known as the Kingfish. I served as governor from 1928 to 1932.

Who am I? ____________________ ______________________

ANSWERS: 1.Lillian Hellman 2.Dolores Spike 3.Evangeline 4.William Claiborne 5.Louis Armstrong 6.Huey Long

Howling Hurricanes

A hurricane is a violent storm that begins over water, and can have wind speeds of more than 74 miles (110 kilometers) per hour. Hurricanes do sometimes hit Louisiana's coast, and usually between July and September.

Find the names of hurricanes that have blown through or near the Louisiana coast in the last century.

WORD BANK

EDITH
GEORGES
AUDREY
HILDA
BETSY
CAMILLE
DANNY
GILBERT
ANDREW
ELENA
JUAN

G E O R G E S M L C D C B A
B A X O N E M G B L A X N U
E N T E I K A K R E N D K D
D D B C H I L D A D N A R R
I R S S A E M I L Y Y R J E
T E C B E T S Y U T I X U Y
H W X S P R T O L H E L A N
K D C I N G I L B E R T N T
B L E C O S H L C T O N I O
C G L P E L E N A H G Z E L
C U Y A C A M I L L E S C X

Indians in Louisiana

Before the European explorers came, Louisiana was inhabited by people of three Native American language groups.
Draw a line from the tribes to their locations on the map.

- The Chitimacha and Atakapa were the Tunican peoples. They lived along the Gulf Coast.

- The Houma, Choctaw, Acolapissa, and Taensa were the Muskogean peoples. They lived in east central Louisiana, near the Mississippi River.

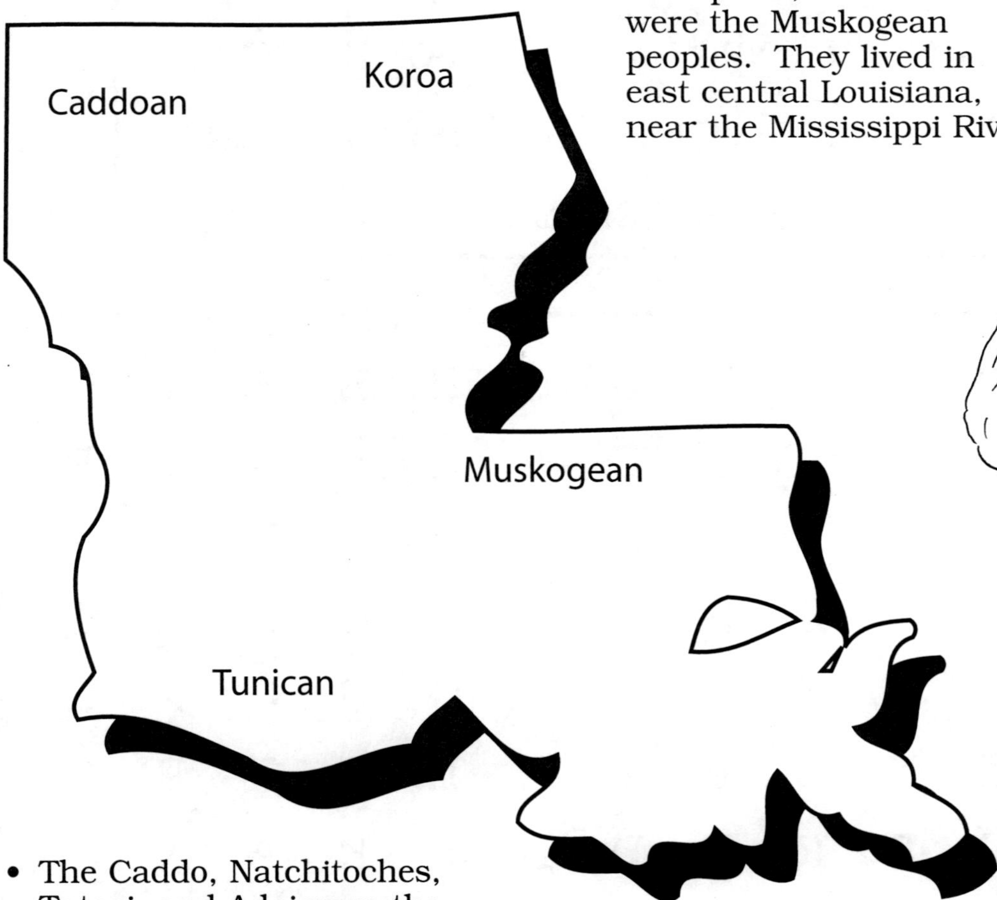

- The Caddo, Natchitoches, Tatasi, and Adai were the Caddoan peoples. They lived in the Northwestern part of the state.

- A small group called the Koroa lived in northeastern Louisiana.

Good Golly! Louisiana Geography Word Search

Find these Louisiana cities in the Word Search!

WORD BANK

SHREVEPORT	RUSTON	ALEXANDRIA
BOSSIER CITY	MONROE	BATON ROUGE
MINDEN	PINEVILLE	NEW ORLEANS
	NATCHITOCHES	

N	A	T	C	H	I	T	O	C	H	E	S	T	O
M	N	E	W	O	R	L	E	A	N	S	X	V	P
I	E	T	V	I	K	M	O	N	R	O	E	C	R
N	R	B	C	R	U	S	T	O	N	M	X	R	I
D	L	S	B	A	T	O	N	R	O	U	G	E	C
E	I	P	I	N	E	V	I	L	L	E	I	P	G
N	N	T	S	P	R	T	D	L	E	R	A	N	N
K	D	C	D	N	C	F	G	N	A	T	M	I	T
B	L	E	A	L	E	X	A	N	D	R	I	A	I
B	O	S	S	I	E	R	C	I	T	Y	A	Y	T
S	H	R	E	V	E	P	O	R	T	X	D	F	C

How Many People in Louisiana?

STATE OF LOUISIANA
CENSUS REPORT

Every ten years, it's time for Louisianians to stand up and be counted. Since 1790, the United States has conducted a census, or count, of each of its citizens. Practice filling out a pretend census form.

Name ______________________________________ Age [ ]

Place of Birth ____

Current Address ____

Does your family own or rent where you live? ____________________

How long have you lived in Louisiana? ______________

How many people are in your family? ______________

How many females? [ ] How many males? [ ]

What are their ages? __________________

How many rooms are in your house? [ ]

How is your home heated? ____________________

How many cars does your family own? [ ]

How many telephones are in your home? [ ]

Is your home a farm? _____________

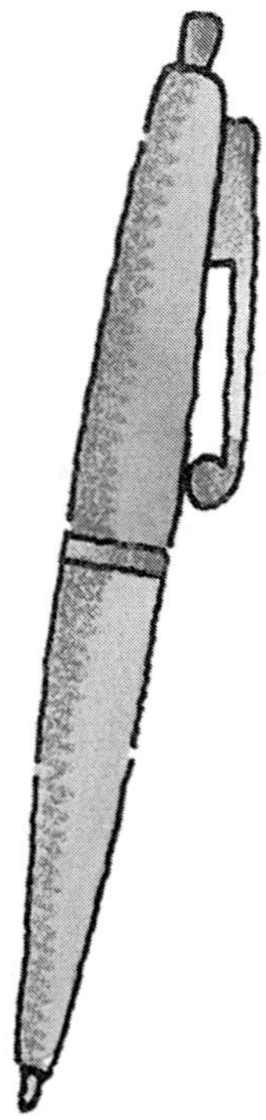

Sounds pretty nosy, doesn't it? But a census is very important. The information is used for all kinds of purposes, including setting budgets, zoning land, determining how many schools to build, and much more. The census helps Louisiana leaders plan for the future needs of its citizens. Hey, that's you!!

Louisiana Cities

Circle Baton Rouge in red. It is Louisiana's state capital.
Circle Shreveport in brown. It is named after a man who broke up a 160 mile (257 kilometer) logjam.
Circle New Orleans in purple. It is where Mardi Gras is held.
Circle Farmerville in green. It is where the D'Arbonne Wildlife Refuge is located.
Add your home city or town if it is not on the map. Circle it in orange. Give it a ☺ to show that you live there.

Oops! The compass rose is missing its cardinal directions. Write N, S, E, W, on the compass rose.

Endangered and Threatened Louisiana

Each state has a list of the endangered species in their state. An animal is labeled endangered when it is in danger of becoming extinct. Land development, changes in climate and weather, and changes in the number of predators are all factors that can cause an animal to become extinct. Today many states are passing laws to help save animals on the endangered species list.

Can you help rescue these endangered and threatened animals by filling in their names below?

1. B ___ ___ C ___ B ___ ___ ___

2. ___ A ___ D E ___ ___ L ___

3. P ___ ___ ___ G ___ I ___ E F ___ L ___ ___ N

4. B ___ ___ ___ N P ___ ___ ___ C ___ N

5. P ___ P ___ ___ G P ___ ___ V ___ ___

Circle the animal that is extinct (not here anymore).

ANSWERS: 1.black bear 2.bald eagle 3.peregrine falcon 4.brown pelican 5.piping plover

Louisiana's State Songs

Louisiana actually has two state songs,
Give Me Louisiana and *You Are My Sunshine*!

Here are the words to *Give Me Louisiana*:

Give me Louisiana, the State where I was born
The State of snowy cotton, the best I've ever known;
A State of sweet magnolias, and Creole melodies.

Oh, give me Louisiana, the State where I was born
Oh, what sweet old mem'ries the mossy old oaks bring.
It brings us the story of our Evangeline.

A State of old tradition, of old plantation days
Makes good ole Louisiana the Sweetest of all States.

Answer the following questions:

1. What are two things that Louisiana is the state of? ____________________ __________________________.
2. What brings sweet memories? __________________________________
3. Whose story does Louisiana bring? ______________________________
4. What makes Louisiana the sweetest state? ________________________

ANSWERS: (may vary slightly) 1.cotton, Creole melodies, old tradition, plantation days 2.mossy old oaks 3.Evangeline 4.old tradition, old plantation days

Getting Ready To Vote

When you turn 18, you will be eligible to vote. Your vote counts! Many elections have been won by just a few votes. The following is a form for your personal voting information. You will need to be a good research student to get all the answers!

I will be eligible to vote on this date: ______________

I live in this Congressional District: ____________

I live in this State Senate District: ______________

I live in this State Representative District: ________

I live in this Voting Precinct: ____________________

The first local election I can vote in will be ________

The first state election I can vote in will be _________

The first national election I can vote in will be _____

The governor of our state is ____________________

One of my state senators is ___________________________________

One of my state representatives is _______________________________

The local public office I would like to run for is ____________________

The state public office I would like to run for is ____________________

The federal public office I would like to run for is ___________________

Louisiana State Seal

The Louisiana state seal was created by William C.C. Claiborne, the first governor of the state. He admired the eastern brown pelican, and was amazed by how it would feed its young. Claiborne started using a seal showing a pelican with three chicks in a nest when he wrote letters. In 1902, it became the official state seal. The seal shows the mother pelican with her babies in gold, surrounded by a blue border. The words "State of Louisiana" are in gold.

Color the state seal.

Animal Scramble

Unscramble the names of these animals you might find in your Louisiana backyard.

Write the answers in the word wheel below the picture of each animal.

1. krtasmu ______________________________
   Hint: She often lives under the ground in river banks.
2. ethiw dleait ered ____________ ______________ ________________
   Hint: He raises the underside of his tail to signal danger!
3. nrcocao ________________________
   Hint: He has very sensitive "fingers" and uses them to find food.
4. nrseare ttoncoliat bitbra ___________ ________________ _________________
   Hint: She would love to eat the cabbages in your garden!
5. yarg lquiersr ____________ ____________________
   Hint: He scurries around all day, burying and digging up food.

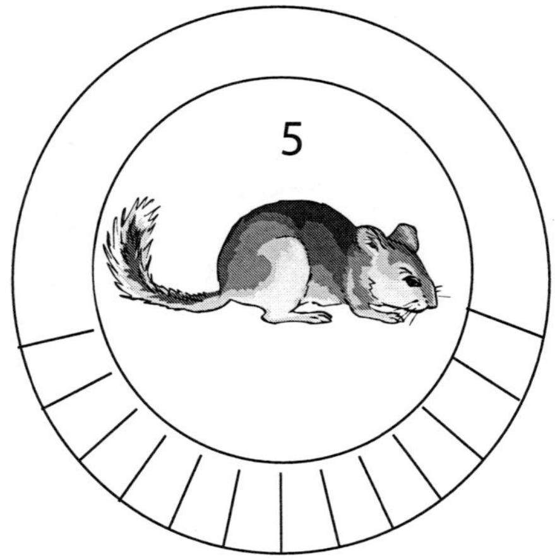

ANSWERS: 1.muskrat 2.white tailed deer 3.raccoon 4.eastern cottontail rabbit 5.gray squirrel

A Quilt of Many Parishes

Louisiana is the only state that is divided into parishes. When Louisiana was a Spanish colony, it was split up into parishes. In 1845, Louisiana's constitution made the parish system official. There are 64 parishes in the state. Every city or town in Louisiana belongs to a parish.

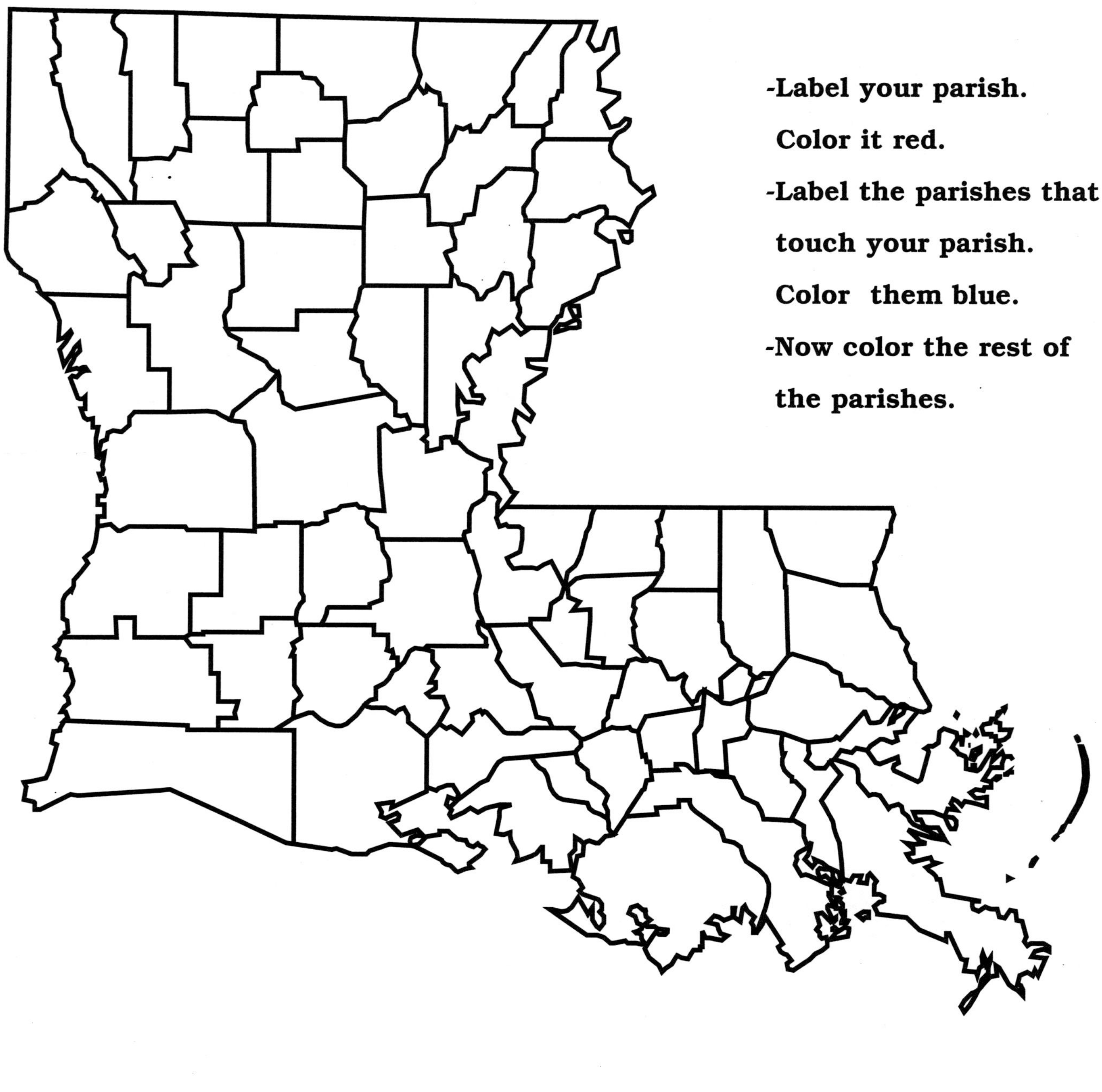

-Label your parish.

Color it red.

-Label the parishes that touch your parish.

Color them blue.

-Now color the rest of the parishes.

Two For The Price Of One!

How many of these two-name places can you match? You might need a map or an atlas to help you figure them out.

1. Abita
2. Alden
3. Baton
4. Bayou
5. Belle
6. Center
7. Cotton
8. Dry
9. East
10. Elm
11. Fort
12. Golden
13. Jean
14. Lake
15. Pleasant

A. Hill
B. Bridge
C. Hodge
D. Lafitte
E. Jesup
F. Creek
G. Barbary
H. Rouge
I. Charles
J. Rose
K. Valley
L. Grove
M. Meadow
N. Point
O. Springs

ANSWERS: 1.O 2.B 3.H 4.G 5.J 6.N 7.K 8.F 9.C 10.L 11.E 12.M 13.D 14.I 15.A

Famous Louisiana African-Americans

Between 1898 and 1954, all schools in Louisiana were segregated. In 1954, the United States Supreme Court ruled that segregation was illegal. In New Orleans two primary schools were integrated in 1960, which caused unrest. But, by the mid 1960s most of Louisiana's schools were no longer segregated. Civil rights were a major issue in Louisiana throughout the 1960s, but by the 1970s many of the problems had been resolved. Many African-Americans made significant contributions to the cause of civil rights and to the state of Louisiana. Below are a few.

Try matching the people with their accomplishments.

1. Alexander Pierre "A.P." Tureaud
2. Kermit A. Parker
3. Ernest Morial
4. Oscar Dunn
5. Louis Armstrong
6. Huey Newton

A. New Orleans civil rights activist

B. famous jazz musician

C. lawyer whose cases helped stop segregation

D. first African-American mayor of New Orleans

E. a New Orleans pharmacist who ran for governor in 1952

F. first African-American lieutenant governor of Louisiana

ANSWERS: 1.C 2.E 3.D 4.F 5.B 6.A

Some Louisiana Firsts

The first two primary schools in New Orleans were opened in 1842. There was one school for boys, and one for girls.

In 1992, the Louisiana Lottery had its first modern drawing.

Jim Halsell, Jr., the first Louisiana astronaut, was launched into space aboard the space shuttle *Columbia* in 1994.

In 1893, the first electric streetcar ran in Baton Rouge.

The first recorded hurricane in Louisiana destroyed New Orleans in 1722.

In 1823, gas lighting was first used in the American Theater of New Orleans.

In 1845, the first free public school was opened in Louisiana.

The first African-American student was admitted to the Louisiana State University's Baton Rouge campus in 1964.

In 1813, William C.C. Claiborne used the pelican and motto as the state seal for the first time.

In 1883, the first train ran from New Orleans to California.

The first rural mail delivery in Louisiana was in 1896.

Can you think of another Louisiana first? Write it down!

____

____

____

Which Founding Person Am I?

From the Word Bank, find my name and fill in the blank.

WORD BANK

John Law
Napoléon Bonaparte
Pierre Le Moyne
Andrew Jackson
Duncan Kenner

1. I was an American general who fought and won the Battle of New Orleans. I may not have been from Louisiana, but I helped save it from the British.

   WHO AM I? ____________ ______________

2. I was a Scottish financier who got King Philippe II's permission to colonize Louisiana. I had to try to trick people to move to the new colony.

   WHO AM I? ____________ ______________

3. I was the leader of France in 1800, and sold Louisiana to the United States for $15 million dollars in 1803.

   WHO AM I? ____________ ______________

4. I was the founder of the Louisiana Sugar Planters Association. I used narrow-gauge railroads to move sugar cane to the mills.

   WHO AM I? ____________ ______________

5. I was a French explorer. In 1699, I founded the royal colony of Louisiana.

   WHO AM I? ____________ __ ____________

ANSWERS: 1.Andrew Jackson 2.John Law 3.Napoléon Bonaparte 4.Duncan Kenner 5. Pierre Le Moyne

It Could Happen– And It Did!

These historical events from Louisiana's past are all out of order.

Can you put them back together in the correct order? (There's a great big hint at the end of each sentence.)

Ernest Morial becomes the first African-American mayor of New Orleans. (1978)

La Salle claims the Louisiana Territory for France. (1682)

Spain gives Louisiana back to France in the Treaty of San Ildefonso. (1800)

The first oil in Louisiana is discovered. (1901)

Louisiana is re-admitted to the Union after the Civil War. (1868)

The first Mardi Gras parade is held in New Orleans. (1838)

Sugar cane is first planted in New Orleans. (1751)

Louisiana becomes the 18th state. (1812)

Andrew Jackson wins the Battle of New Orleans. (1815)

New Orleans is founded. (1718)

1. ______________________________

2. ______________________________

3. ______________________________

4. ______________________________

5. ______________________________

6. ______________________________

7. ______________________________

8. ______________________________

9. ______________________________

10. ______________________________

Louisiana People

A state is not just towns and mountains and rivers. A state is its people! But the really important people in a state are not always famous. You may know them—they may be your mom, your dad, or your teacher. The average, everyday person is the one who helps to make the state a good state. How? By working hard, by paying taxes, by voting, and by helping Louisiana children grow up to be good state citizens!

Match each Louisiana person with their accomplishment.

1. Louis Armstrong
2. John James Audubon
3. Lillian Hellman
4. Huey Pierce Long
5. Edward Douglass White
6. John Hays
7. William C.C. Claiborne
8. Alexander Pierre Tureaud

A. famous New Orleans playwright
B. inventor of Tabasco hot sauce
C. first governor of the state of Louisiana
D. civil rights activist
E. governor known as the Kingfish
F. famous birdwatcher, author, and artist
G. famous jazz musician
H. United States Supreme Court justice

ANSWERS: 1.G 2.F 3.A 4.E 5.H 6.B 7.C 8.D

Similar Symbols

Louisiana has many state symbols including a state bird, flag, flower, and even crustacean! Circle the item below that is not a symbol of Louisiana.

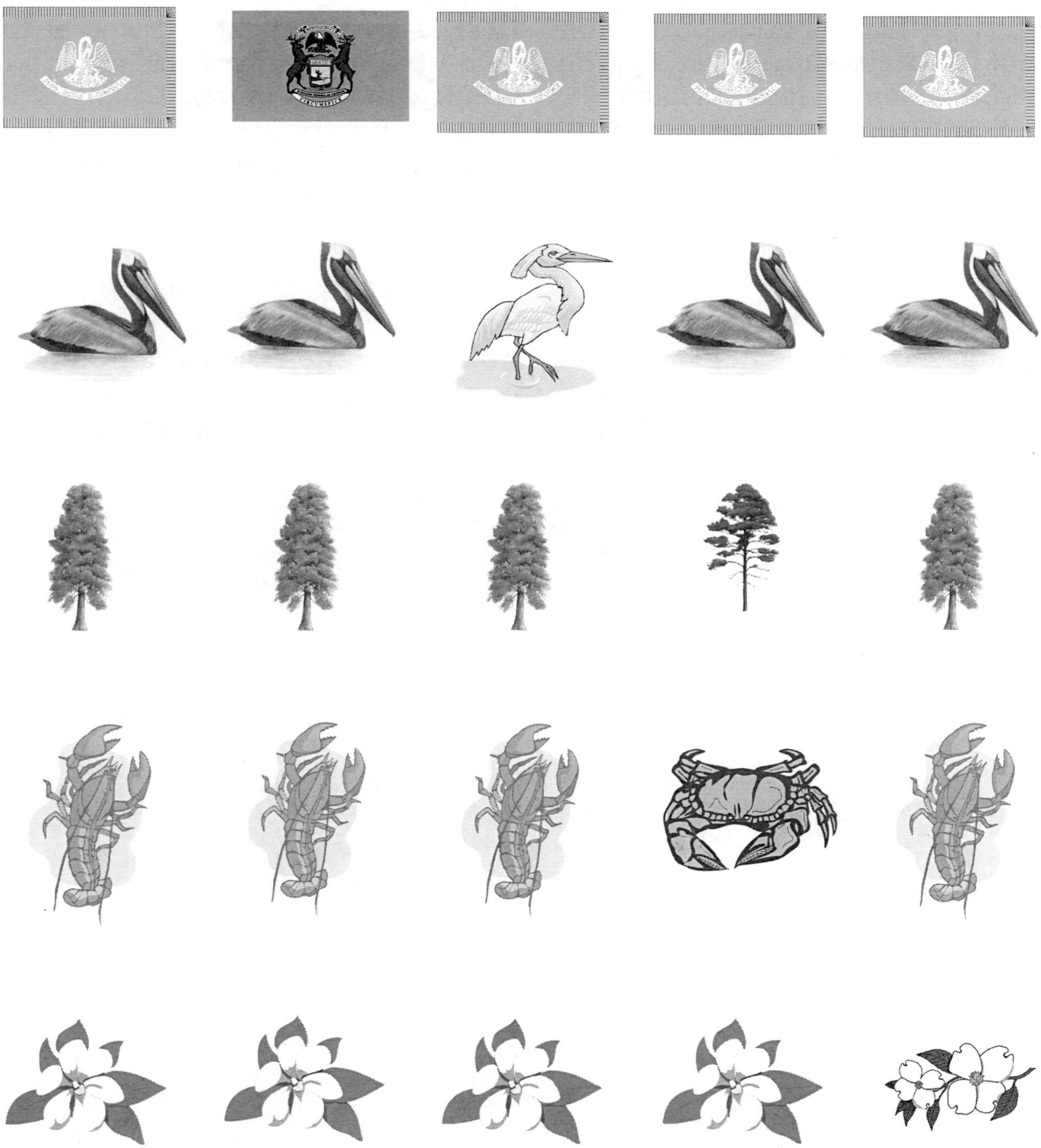

Mounds Abound in Louisiana

People have lived in Louisiana for thousands of years. Some of these people built earthen mounds of different sizes all over the state. Some of the mounds were shaped like pyramids and used as temples. One group of mounds found in Louisiana is the effigy mound, shaped like birds, animals, and even people. Scientists believe that these mounds may have marked the boundaries of the Indians' territories. Many of the mounds have been destroyed by scavengers looking for treasure.

You are an archaeologist digging into one of the Louisiana mounds. What kind of artifacts do you think you'll find? Draw the treasures you unearth in the space below. Make sure you label what they are!

Louisiana Economy Word Wheel

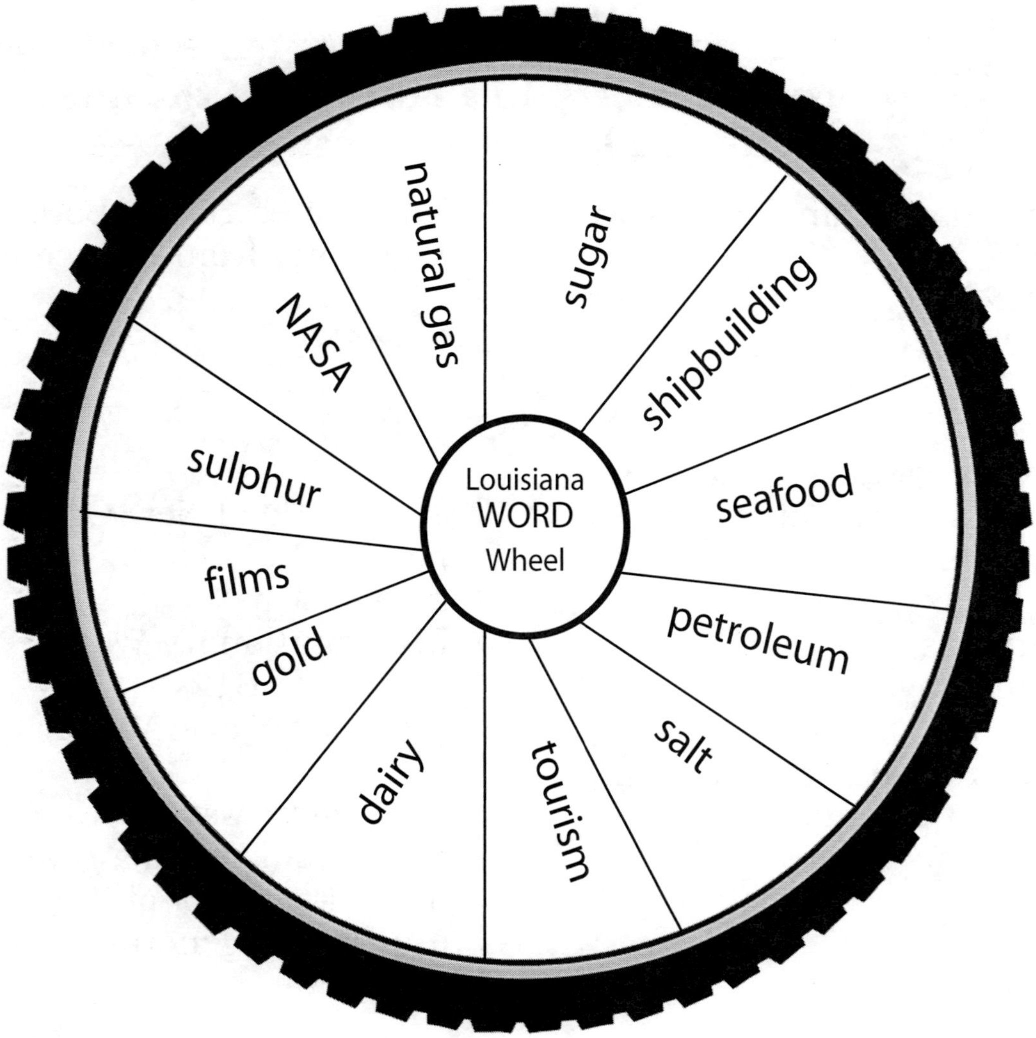

1. One major element of Louisiana's economy is ____________________ refining.
2. Louisiana produces just over one-quarter of the United States' _______ ______ supplies.
3. Several _________ mines in Louisiana provide this popular seasoning.
4. Because Louisiana has so many ports, ____________________ is a major source of income.
5. Louisiana is the second largest producer of _______ cane in the U.S.
6. About 25 percent of all the ________________ in the United States is caught by Louisiana's fishing industry.
7. Martin Marietta in New Orleans manufactures the external fuel tanks for _________'s space shuttle program.
8. The ______________ industry is important in Louisiana, and many movies have been filmed there.
9. Louisiana is full of sights and attractions that make _________ a huge part of the economy.
10. The first _______________ ever mined in America was dug up in Louisiana.

ANSWERS: 1.petroleum 2.natural gas 3.salt 4.shipbuilding 5.sugar 6.seafood 7.NASA 8.film 9.tourism 10.sulphur

Know your Louisiana Facts!

Pop quiz! It's time to test your knowledge of Louisiana! Try to answer all of the questions before you look at the answers.

1. Louisiana became a state in
   - ❍ a. 1812
   - ❍ b. 1912
   - ❍ c. 1902
   - ❍ d. 1972

2. The descendants of Acadian colonists in Louisiana are the
   - ❍ a. Creoles
   - ❍ b. Cajuns
   - ❍ c. Parishes
   - ❍ d. Jambalayas

3. Louisiana was originally a(n) ________ colony.
   - ❍ a. English
   - ❍ b. German
   - ❍ c. French
   - ❍ d. American

4. The largest city in Louisiana is
   - ❍ a. Baton Rouge
   - ❍ b. Shreveport
   - ❍ c. Alexandria
   - ❍ d. New Orleans

5. The capital of Louisiana is
   - ❍ a. Baton Rouge
   - ❍ b. New Orleans
   - ❍ c. Alexandria
   - ❍ d. Shreveport

6. The United States bought Louisiana from France in
   - ❍ a. 1803
   - ❍ b. 1848
   - ❍ c. 1812
   - ❍ d. 1815

7. The Battle of New Orleans was part of the
   - ❍ a. Civil War
   - ❍ b. Revolutionary War
   - ❍ c. War of 1812
   - ❍ d. second World War

8. Jean Lafitte was
   - ❍ a. the first Louisiana governor
   - ❍ b. the first mayor of New Orleans
   - ❍ c. a British general
   - ❍ d. a pirate

9. You would find the French Quarter in
   - ❍ a. New Orleans
   - ❍ b. Baton Rouge
   - ❍ c. Alexandria
   - ❍ d. Natchitoches

10. Louisiana's state seal was adopted in
    - ❍ a. 1802
    - ❍ b. 1902
    - ❍ c. 1702
    - ❍ d. 1812

ANSWERS: 1.a 2.b 3.c 4.d 5.a 6.a 7.c 8.d 9.a 10.b

Scavenger Hunt Louisiana Style

This is a fun hunt that includes your friends or classmates. Read the list below, find someone who has "been there and done that," get their signature and move on to the next item on your list. See how fast you can complete the scavenger hunt. Have your teacher, or parent, check the answers to Part 2.

Part 1
<u>Find someone who has:</u>

been to the state capitol building____________________________

seen a brown pelican____________________________________

visited the French Quarter________________________________

attended Mardi Gras_____________________________________

been to the Louisiana Superdome___________________________

seen a hurricane____

Part 2
<u>Find somone who can:</u>

tell you Louisiana's statehood date__________________________

say the state motto______________________________________

name the state capital___________________________________

tell you who Huey Long was_______________________________

name a major Louisiana river______________________________

name the governor of Louisiana____________________________

name the state tree_______________________________________

Our Cities, Our Towns

Many cities in Louisiana are famous for one or more things.
Match the city with something that it is known for!

1. Monroe	A. home of Jim Bowie
2. Farmerville	B. named after a man who broke up a logjam
3. Shreveport	C. capital of Louisiana
4. Baton Rouge	D. Capital of the Cajun Prairie
5. Ville Platte	E. Louisiana Cotton Festival
6. Eunice	F. the Live Oak Society
7. Opelousas	G. the Biedenharn Bible Research Museum
8. Lafayette	H. D'Arbonne National Wildlife Refuge

ANSWERS: 1.G 2.H 3.B 4.C 5.E 6.D 7.A 8.F

Red Beans and Rice!

Many of Lousiana's foods are spicy and hot, especially the Cajun recipes. Here's a simple recipe for one of them.

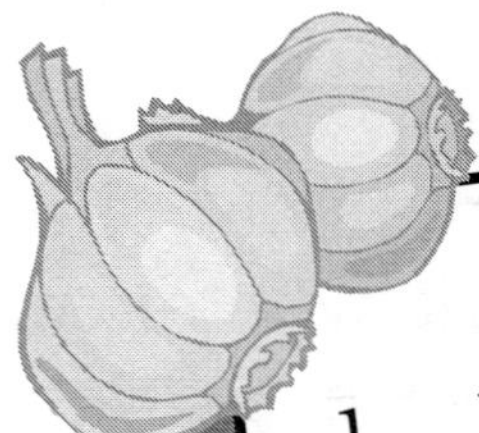

Ingredients:

1. 1 pound (0.45 kilogram) dried kidney beans
2. oil
3. 1 large onion, chopped
4. 1 green pepper, chopped
5. 4 celery stalks, chopped
6. 4 cloves of garlic, minced
7. 1 smoked ham hock
8. 1/2 to 1 pound (0.225 to 0.45 kilogram) andouille sausage
9. 1 bay leaf
10. salt, cayenne, Tabasco sauce, black pepper to taste

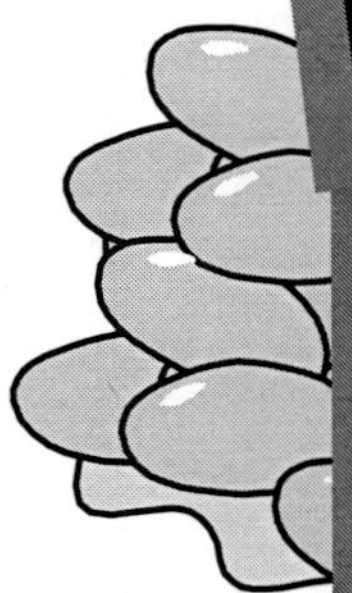

Directions:

1. Wash and soak the beans overnight.
2. Drain the beans and cover them in water. Boil them for 45-60 minutes or until the beans are tender.
3. Sauté the onion, green pepper, garlic, and celery in the oil. Add the garlic and sauté for one minute.
4. Drain and return the beans to the pot, add the vegetables and ham hock, sausage, bay leaf, cayenne, black pepper, salt, and Tabasco sauce. Add enough water to cover the mixture
5. Boil the mixture. Reduce the temperature and cover the pot. Simmer for about 3 hours, until the mixture is thick.
6. Serve over hot white rice, and add as much Tabasco sauce as you can stand!

The Atchafalaya Swamp

"Atchafalaya" means "long river" in the language of the Atakapa Indians who once lived in Louisiana. This flowage carries more than 1.3 billion gallons (4.9 billion liters) of water a day. Soil in the water has built up and changed how the river has looked over the past 60 years. The landscape fluctuates constantly, when islands are built up, lakes fill, and the river channels change direction. There are many marshes and wetlands in the area, and they are full of wildlife!

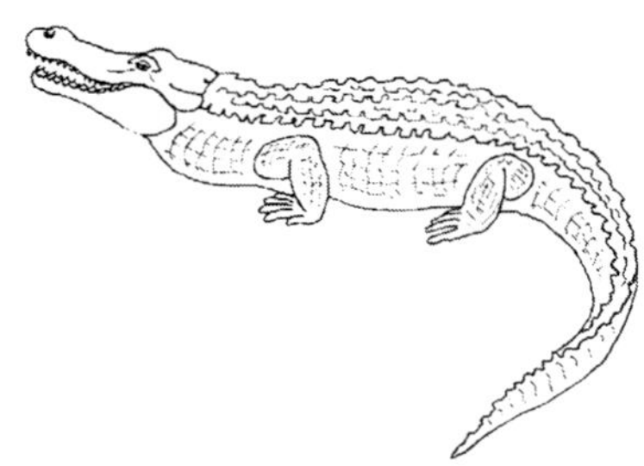

A *haiku* is a three line poem with a certain number of syllables in each line. Look at the example below:

The first line has 5 syllables: At/cha/fa/lay/a
1 2 3 4 5

The second line has 7 syllables: Full of beau/ti/ful mar/shes
1 2 3 4 5 6 7

The third line has 5 syllables: An/i/mals call home.
1 2 3 4 5

Now, write your own haiku about the Atchafalaya Swamp!

____

____

____

Gulf Habitat

Why do sea animals live where they do?

Sea animals need good surroundings just like we do! The Gulf of Mexico provides a wonderful environment for all types of sea animals. At times, to the sea animals, the water can seem like a vast bowl of soup. Sometimes you can see dolphins in a feeding frenzy. They surface for air and dive for food. Eating is not the only thing that determines where sea animals live. Temperature, salinity, and breeding habitat all affect where sea animals live.

Use numbers (1-10) to put the following sea animals in alphabetical order.

_____skate

_____dolphin

_____tarpon

_____shark

_____eel

_____ray

_____squid

_____tuna

_____turtle

_____blue marlin

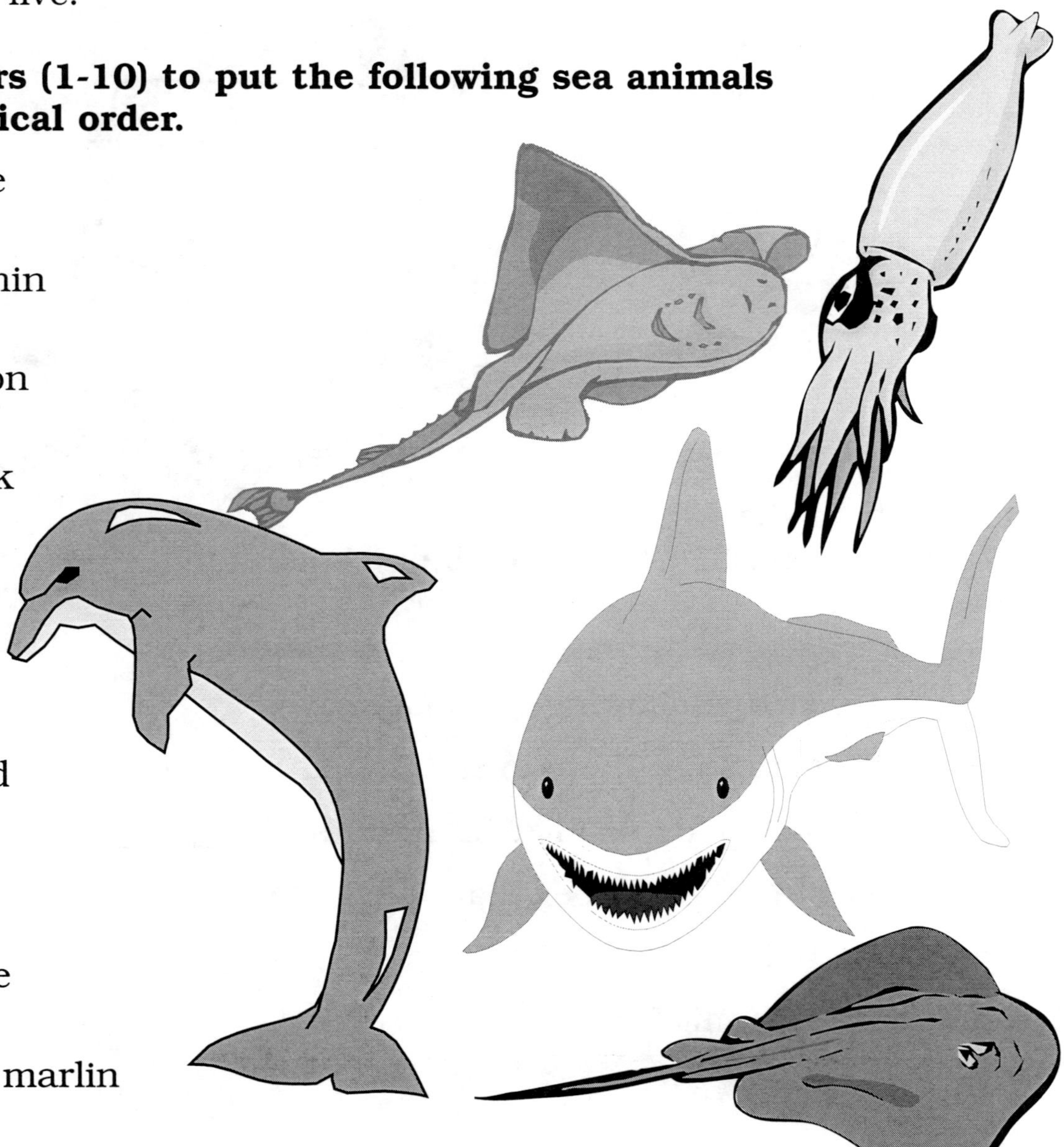

ANSWERS: 1.blue marlin 2.dolphin 3.eel 4.ray 5.shark 6.skate 7.squid 8.tarpon 9.tuna 10.turtle

How Big is Louisiana?

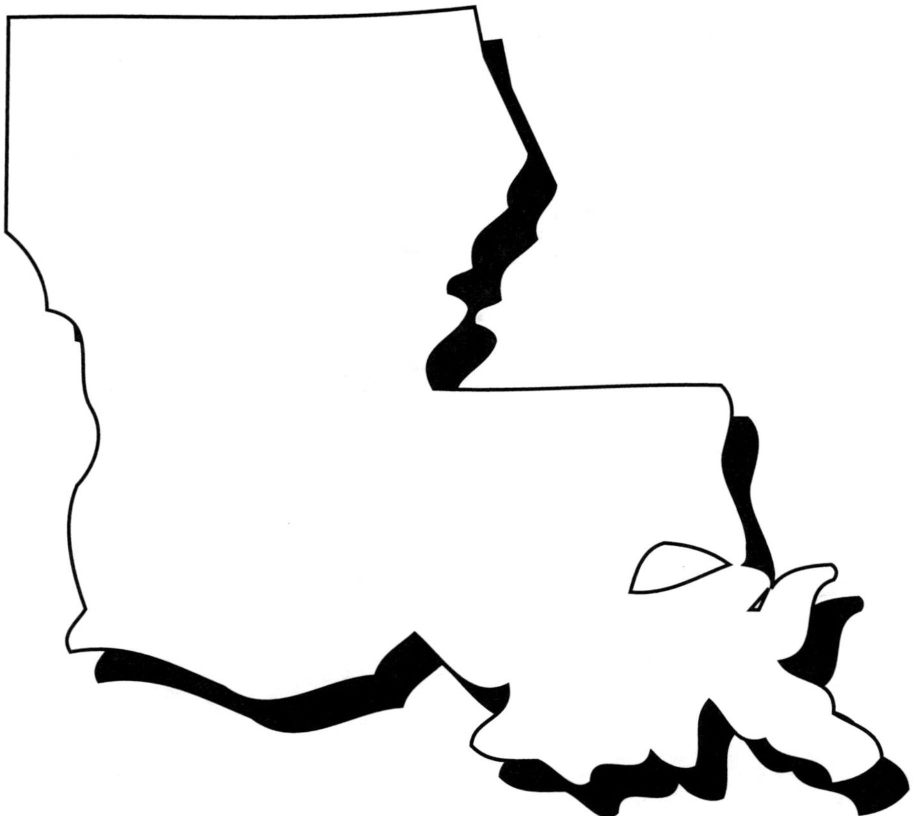

Louisiana is the 31st largest state in the United States. It has an area of 49,650 square miles (128,593 square kilometers).

Can you answer the following questions?

1. How many states are there in the United States? ___________
2. This many states are smaller than our state: _______________
3. This many states are larger than our state: ________________
4. One mile = 5,280 ___ ___ ___ ___
5. Draw a "square mile" below.

ANSWERS: 1.50 2.19 3.30 4.feet 5. ☐

Louisiana's National Parks

Louisiana has several national parks, and one national forest. Each of these attractions is devoted to preserving Louisiana life, environment, and culture.

WORD BANK

New Orleans Jazz	Cane River
Kisatchie	Poverty Point
Jean Lafitte	Vicksburg

Unscramble the names of these National Parks found in Louisiana. Use the Word Bank to help you.

1. N E A C E V R R I __________ __________________

2. E A J N E F I T L A T ___________ _________________

3. W N E R O L A E S N A Z J Z _____ ________ ____________

4. K I V C S R G U B _______________________

5. V T R E O P Y N I T P O __________ __________________

6. T E S K A C I H I __________________________

ANSWERS: 1.Cane River 2.Jean Lafitte 3.New Orleans Jazz 4.Vicksburg 5.Poverty Point 6.Kisatchie

L is for Louisiana

L is for Lafitte the pirate

O is for Opelousa, home of Jim Bowie

U is for unbelievable food

I is for Indians of many tribes

S is for spicy Creole cuisine

I is for industrial powerhouse

A is for Acadian ancestry

N is for New Orleans

A is for Avery Island